Praise for William J. Elliott

"'If God is holding me, why am I holding on?' is the central question Bill Elliott answers in his sanity—defying journey into the Judean desert. After forty days and nights in the place where Jesus wrestled with demons and came home to God, Elliott recounts how he too fell into the Divine. Few stories are as transforming as *Falling into the Face of God*."

—HUGH PRATHER, AUTHOR OF *NOTES TO MYSELF*

"This invaluable record deserves to be a bestseller, not only for its inherent wisdom but also for its clarity and respect for the many ways there are to be and to believe."

—PUBLISHERS WEEKLY, ON *TYING ROCKS TO CLOUDS*

"... an utterly winsome book, one that will win a special place in readers' hearts ... It's not just the wise and spiritual things his respondents say that make it sing—it's the search that Bill Elliott undertook and his bold idea of finding wisdom by simply asking. By the book's end, Elliott is wiser, more spiritual. So will be many of his readers."

—BOOKLIST, ON *TYING ROCKS TO CLOUDS*

"A treasury of talks about the treasure of life, the great hidden pearl that is out there right in the open."

—BOOK READER, ON *TYING ROCKS TO CLOUDS*

Falling into the
Face of God

Falling into the Face of God

*Forty Days and Nights in
the Judean Desert*

WILLIAM J. ELLIOTT

W PUBLISHING GROUP
A Division of Thomas Nelson Publishers
Since 1798

www.wpublishinggroup.com

Published by W Publishing Group, a Division of Thomas Nelson, Inc., P.O. Box 141000, Nashville, Tennessee 37214.

W Publishing Group books may be purchased in bulk for educational, business, fund-raising, or sales promotional use. For information, please e-mail SpecialMarkets@ThomasNelson.com.

All Scripture quotations, unless otherwise indicated, are taken from the Holy Bible, New International Version (NIV). Copyright © 1973, 1978, 1984, International Bible Society. Used by permission of Zondervan.

Other Scripture references are from the following sources:
The King James Version (KJV); The Message (MSG), copyright © 1993. Used by permission of Nav Press Publishing Group; New American Standard Bible (NASB), © 1960, 1977, 1995 by the Lockman Foundation; the New King James Version (NKJV®), copyright © 1979, 1980, 1982, Thomas Nelson, Inc., Publishers; the *Holy Bible*, New Living Translation (NLT), copyright © 1996. Used by permission of Tyndale House Publishers, Inc., Wheaton, Illinois 60189. All rights reserved.

Page Design: Stacy Clark

Library of Congress Cataloging-in-Publication Data

Elliott, William, 1959–
    Falling into the face of God : forty days and nights in the Judean desert / William J. Elliott.
    p. cm.
    ISBN 0-8499-0071-9
    1. Elliott, William, 1959– 2. Christian biography—United States. 3. Mental health personnel—United States—Biography. I. Title.
    BR1725.E465A3 2006
    275.694'9083092—dc22

                                    2005030488

Printed in the United States of America
06 07 08 09 10 QW 9 8 7 6 5 4 3 2 1

At once the Spirit sent him out into the desert,
and he was in the desert forty days, being tempted
by Satan. He was with the wild animals,
and angels attended him.

—Mark 1:12–14

If there is any peace it will come through being,
not having.

—Henry Miller

You cannot see My face,
for no man can see Me and live!

—God to Moses, Exodus 33:20 NASB

Contemplatives and ascetics of all ages and religions
have sought God in the silence and solitude of the
desert, forest, and mountain.

—Mother Teresa

For those who seek union with God, the Beloved and Supreme Being.

arrival

METSOKEY-DERAGOT HOSTEL
JUDEAN DESERT, ISRAEL

In early June of 2002, I left the United States and traveled to the locus of my own soul. If one were to look at a map, they would say that my destination was Israel (specifically the Judean desert) and that I had traveled 6,497 miles. But in actuality, I traveled much farther than that—upon a road whose traversing is measured not in miles, but by the deepening of human experience, love, and acceptance; and not by direction (for there is only one direction—inward). And whose perilous mountains, cliffs, and valleys were composed not of stone or sand, but of one's own psyche (the most dangerous of the world's creations).

"You're making a mistake," said Orel, the manager of the Metsokey-Deragot Hostel. "You've got snakes and scorpions out in the desert, and it's very hot, and there are so many cliffs where you can fall . . . so many things that can go wrong," he said, shaking his head in disbelief, "and there will be no one to help you if you fall or get bitten by a snake and can't contact us."

Orel was right; I could easily die out in the desert. I knew almost nothing about being in nature. I ventured into nature only occasionally—and that was to play golf. The Metsokey-Deragot Hostel was in the middle of the Judean desert, miles away from any town. And once I ventured out into the desert, I would be miles from Metsokey-Deragot.

I looked over at Ya'el for some kind of assurance. She was the girlfriend of Tamir, the guide who had found a place for me in the Judean desert. But since he had punctured his eardrum the day before, it was she who would be dropping me off near my destination. Ya'el wouldn't even look at me. Instead, she looked down at the floor and nodded in agreement with Orel.

I turned away from them and looked out the office window into the desert. At one time the Metsokey-Deragot Hostel had been a *kibbutz*, started by Jewish hippies. But eventually they realized that nothing would grow here, so they abandoned it, leaving four or five small adobe buildings. It was now a place where tourists occasionally came to spend time in the desert. But anyone who had ever been in the desert (in the way that the desert demanded) knew that this wasn't really "the desert." Instead, the desert was still out there, beyond the barbed-wire fence that lay broken and unmended. Beyond the several sets of small hills that distanced one from the safety of others. Beyond the space that opened up just past those same hills, a space so hungry for disturbance or anomaly that it would swallow up any call for help before it reached its recipient. In a science-fiction novel, the Metsokey-Deragot Hostel would be the last space outpost, the place from which the hero or fool sets off as he ventures into the vast unknown.

"And the scorpions are nasty," a voice with a British accent said from behind the counter.

I turned to see a wisp of a woman with short, multicolored hair, a pierced nose, and sad, droopy eyes. Her name was Kate.

"I picked up a box one day," Kate said, "and there were twenty scorpions under it. They scattered. I jumped up and down, but one of the little suckers stung me. If a scorpion gets you in the leg, you'll have almighty pain for seven hours. But the legs and arms are the best places to get stung because the lymph nodes can stop the poison from reaching the heart. If you get stung in the throat or chest, the poison goes right to the heart and can give you a heart attack. I even felt my heart shudder a bit when I was stung."

"So you see," Orel said, "it's not just me saying how dangerous it is in the desert. Why don't you set up your tent just over the first hill? No one will bother you there, and we will still be close enough to help you. I'm not saying any of this to get you to stay at our hostel and pay. It's just that what you're doing is very, very dangerous."

As I walked back to my room at the hostel, I was scared. Orel, Ya'el, and Kate had added fear to the doubts I already had. I didn't want to die in the desert—that's for sure. I'd be embarrassed to die in the desert! To throw away my life like that . . . But what was I going to do? I was called into the desert, led there by the Spirit of God—at least that's how it felt to me. It was as though my life (or a part of me) was already in the desert, waiting for the rest of me to come and claim it. Was I going to say no to the Spirit of God? No to my life? That night, as I lay in bed, I prayed to God to stop me if I was doing something stupid. After I was done praying, the reality of what I was about to do hit me.

"I'm going to be alone in the desert for forty days," I said aloud.

I laughed at how ridiculous it all sounded, and in the midst of my laughter, I had the strange feeling that I was falling. And then I remembered *him*.

Fifteen years ago, I lived on a hill in a Tibetan monastery just outside Katmandu. On a black-as-coal night, I stood in front of a roaring fire lit by the western monks who gathered each night about halfway down the hill on the eastern edge of the monastic grounds. It was my first time there, and I was invited to the fire by a crazy Australian.

"Bill," the crazy Australian said as we stood around the fire, "people are born with a wound that time sliced open, a pain that goes from their throat to their belly. They either spend their whole life trying to avoid it or trying to understand it. I've got you pegged as trying to understand it.

"But," he added, laughing, "you haven't got any idea what you're in for, do you, mate?"

That was fifteen years ago, and for a moment when he said that, I felt as if I were falling, but I just smiled and stared into the flames. I was happy then. I had discovered Buddhism, lamas, mantras, and dark nights around the fire. And then there was the crazy Australian. He was in his midforties, slim, with dark brown eyes and hair.

He had a habit of irritating people by seeing, and then verbalizing, their deepest secrets. For example, once when we were seated at lunch, he turned to a Dutch man and asked, "How's your heroin addiction?"

There was an awkward silence, and then the eyes of the Dutchman narrowed to slits. "How did you know about that?" he asked.

"Aw, mate," the Australian replied, "I can see the anguish on your face."

Because of his piercing insight, whenever the Australian opened his mouth, everyone scattered—except me. I'm not sure why I didn't run away; maybe it was because I partly understood what he was talking about. Or maybe it was because he said I was one of the few people in that monastery who knew anything, and I liked that. Or maybe it was his wild aliveness and unpredictability that seemed to have so much more freedom than the meditative control I was trying to exert over my life. All I knew was that he went wherever he wanted, and I don't mean cities or countries; I mean soul places. He traveled to every corner of his soul—places I had been afraid to go.

And now, fifteen years later, the night before I was to go out into the desert, I remembered him—and I wasn't really sure why.

I had a vivid dream about Christian monks. In it, three of them were called away from their monastery. They went into a large hall filled with other monks, where there was a monk laid out in a coffin. He was old and had died. He was the head monk, the abbot and spiritual father. All the other monks were paying respects.

Suddenly I became one of the three monks, and I realized that we were now the most senior monks in the monastery. We went to the front of the line and stood before the casket. The dream changed, and I was talking from a pew. It was an inspired speech.

"The purpose of attaining spiritual awareness," I said, "is so that people can be creative. And the purpose of those who try to be creative is to be spiritually aware. But most of those who try to be aware are never actually creative." (I could feel the other monks' disapproval as I said this.) "And those who are creative are rarely aware," I continued. "Instead, they become the kind who drink too much, who use and abuse people. We need to be both aware *and* creative—with compassion and love. And if we can't be compassionate, then at least we can be open to being so."

I stopped and sat down. A friend next to me asked if I was concerned that I spoke well. I said, "No—it was great." And I knew it was, because I wasn't speaking from ego—I was speaking from Spirit.

I put my arms up on the pew in front of me and bowed my head. I cried out. A gigantic energy was released, and I felt blessed in God's presence. I walked out into the street. I felt as if I was finished with something.

Then I saw an old friend walking on the other side of the street. "Are you still a monk?" I called to him.

He turned, and I saw that he was wearing a tuxedo. He came over to me.

"Will you walk with me?" I asked. "I want to talk."

"I love you so much," he replied, "and you have always been my boss."

As we walked, we talked about the possibility of my leaving the monkhood. At times we hugged and cried. And so the dream ended.

After waking up at about 5:00 a.m., I got out of bed and dressed quietly. Once outside, I was immediately struck by the beauty of the desert in the morning; the landscape and sky a mixture of brown, pink, and blue. A cool wind blew lightly across my skin. The moon was full.

I climbed up a small hill, sat on a stone ledge, and waited for the sun to rise. To my right, about 150 yards away, a group of people also seemed to be waiting for the sunrise. As I watched them, it hit me—I was lonely. I wished they'd invite me over to talk with them. But I was going to be away from people for the next forty days. I'd better get used to being alone.

day 1

The stones and gravel crunched beneath the tires as the car slowly drove away. First driving over one hill, then another, before finally disappearing over the third. I swallowed hard. The doorway through which I entered the Judean desert had closed—actualy, it was more than closed—*it was gone.* I sighed deeply and turned to carry more than four hundred pounds of gear and water to my as-yet-unknown campsite. A large black beetle crawled by.

"Well, what do you think of my being here?" I asked. He didn't reply; he just moved along as though he had never heard me.

I turned to the desert itself, looked at its wide-open space with its rolling brown and tan hills.

"Well," I said, "what do you have to say?"

"We've seen many of your kind," the hills replied.

"So what can you teach me?" I asked.

This time the hills were silent.

"Why are you going to the desert?" my brother had asked on the phone a few days before I left.

"I'll tell you when we meet at O'Hare," I said.

In the past, whenever I've tried to tell my brother—a fifty-six-year-old ex-cop, husband, father of four, and survivor of two heart attacks—about my spiritual pursuits, I've lost him pretty quickly. And it's not because he isn't wise. It's just because it's not his way.

"Bill," he once told me, "I come home from work and all my kids come running and say, 'Daddy, Daddy'—and I feel so good. That's all I need."

Once he even suggested I find a woman and "get her pregnant—then you'll be fine."

My brother had one existential crisis in his life. He was twenty-three years old, married, had a kid on the way, and our parents were sick.

"I was just really anxious," he told me. "I thought I was losing it."

So he went to the only "religious" person he knew—Father John Sherry. The good father invited my brother in, and they sat down in the priest's living room. My brother explained everything to Father Sherry, and then Father Sherry stood up and went into the other room, saying, "I've got just the thing for you."

My brother at one time wanted to be a priest. When I asked him why, he said, "Because they were always playing basketball with the kids, and I liked the thought of getting paid to play basketball."

So when Father Sherry went into the other room to get my brother the answer to his problem, my brother got worried.

Oh no, he thought. *He's going to come back with a Bible and give me religion.*

Father Sherry came back with a whiskey on the rocks.

"Here, drink this," he said, "and everything will be all right."

And you know what? For my brother, everything *was* all right after that.

When I finally met my brother at the airport McDonald's an hour before my flight left for Israel, he didn't ask why I was going to the desert. Instead, he brought along a Ping Putter someone had given him.

"What do you think of this, brother Bill?" he asked.

I took the putter in my hands, made a few practice putts with it, and then pronounced it a great putter. My brother had recently retired and taken up golf. Since he knew I was into golf—well, I guess that was easier for him to talk about than the possibility that something might happen to me in the desert. We made small talk while sharing fries and a cheeseburger.

"Well, brother Jim," I said, standing up, "if something happens to me—I love you a lot."

"Hey," he said abruptly, "I already told you I loved you back when I had my heart attack. So if something happens—I already said it."

So his question remained unanswered: Why was I going to the desert?

The most obvious reason for going into the desert for forty days was because Jesus did, and my connection to Jesus had become very strong during the past five years while writing a book about him titled *A Place at the Table*. And like Jesus, when God says, "You are my son, whom I love," the love shoots up from within your soul and affects everything you do. I went into the desert because I felt that love and I heard those words, and now I longed to relax into them, to allow them to overcome and overtake me, to feel them all the way down into the grounded feet of the soul. Just as an engaged couple's next step is marriage, my going to the desert was the next step in my relationship with God. And this relationship demanded a consummation; a confrontation of both love and anger that could not be avoided any longer. And I didn't want any interruptions: no television, no friends, no lovers, nothing that had to be done other than eat, sleep, go to the toilet, and relate to God.

And yet there was a simpler, truer, and deeper reason for my going into the desert: *I was called into the desert*. My job was to get myself there with as few expectations as possible, then allow the desert, God, and the Spirit to show me why I had come.

I picked up a five-gallon jug of water and started the trek through a dry riverbed to my campsite. Actually, I didn't have a campsite yet; I just knew that I had the whole desert to pitch my tent in, and that at the end of this riverbed (or *wadi*) there was a canyon that opened to the Dead Sea. In the canyon was a small cave about a twenty-foot climb down from the plateau. As I walked along, I spontaneously started to sing, "Yashafi, Yakafi." I wasn't sure what it meant; I just knew it was a Sufi *wasifa* (or "prayer")—and I trusted that my soul knew what it meant. My singing was a way of announcing my presence, and I felt the Spirit all around me as I sang. My singing transformed the exhausting work of carrying the five-gallon water jugs and eighty-pound duffel bags in the 125-degree midday heat into something joyful.

By the time I found a spot for my tent on the plateau above the canyon, it was already three thirty in the afternoon. I chose the plateau because my image of the desert wasn't one of canyons, cliffs, and rocky formations. Instead, I had imagined the desert to be a sandy, wide-open space with dunes that constantly changed shape due to the shifting winds. In that space I had seen myself wearing flowing robes like Peter O'Toole in *Lawrence of Arabia,* and communing with God like Jesus.

Despite being exhausted, I hurriedly set up my tent while anticipating the relaxation and comfort that would come from being able to plop down on the floor of my tent once it was up. Since I had heard horror stories about both scorpions and snakes, I took the precaution of putting down two tarps: one under the tent and one on the floor inside the tent. My thinking was that if a snake or scorpion crawled under my tent and I stepped on it, a stinger or a set of fangs wouldn't be able to bite or sting through three layers of thick plastic.

The tent was a white-and-green four-person dome tent. I didn't know why they called it a "four-person tent," because it wasn't much more than six feet in diameter, and there was no way four people could live in the thing without driving one another nuts. I bought the tent almost ten years ago for around a hundred bucks. Back then, I fantasized about becoming a camper and an outdoorsman who wore flannel shirts and woke up with the rising sun. The fantasy never materialized, because I like being comfortable too much, and the outdoors was almost never as comfortable as the indoors. It was usually too hot or too cold outside, while inside I could usually just adjust the thermostat to make it perfect. There were always bugs outside—whether it was mosquitoes or gnats or flies or yellow jackets or ants—you get the idea. Whereas indoors, there were seldom any bugs—and the few that made it inside I could kill.

Then, of course, I could always lie on my couch when I was at home and watch television, and that was more comfortable than anyplace you'll find camping, because when camping there's always at least one rock or stone or bump to spoil the perfect spot. But now my house, my couch, and my thermostat were all thousands of miles away, and this tent, with its zippered screen flap and quarter-inch foam mat thrown on the floor, was my only comfort. As soon as the tent was up, I threw all my gear inside, drank some water, and lay down, exhausted.

After fifteen minutes or so, it dawned on me that I wasn't comfortable yet. But I was lying down, wasn't I? Actually, I was sweating more than when I had been outside, but that was impossible, because it was more than 125 degrees outside, and . . .

Then I realized, *It's hotter inside the tent than it is outside!*

"In the desert," Tamir, my desert guide, had said only a few days before, "a tent is fiction."

I had, of course, heard him say this, but I'm a stubborn man. And since I had never been in the desert, I assumed I could make a tent be nonfiction. But the desert was introducing to me my first lesson, which was that the simple but piercingly real and overwhelmingly powerful experience of life in the desert will burn away any and all pretense of knowing what one doesn't really know.

"I guess he was sort of right," I said under my breath as I sat up in my tent and sighed. *The cave should be cooler*, I thought. *I can rest there.* I stood up and went outside, zipping up the tent behind me. I walked toward the cave but got only a few yards away before I stopped in midstride. *What about the scorpions? Did I zip the tent all the way? What if I left the zipper just a little bit unzipped, and a scorpion got in, and it's lying under my sheets or in my sleeping bag or in my duffel bag or in* . . . It could be in anything, waiting for that moment when I reached under or into something or . . .

I turned around and walked back to the tent. I double-checked the zipper and pulled it closed as much as possible. But there was still a little space where *something could get in.* There must be a foolproof method, a way to assure myself there wouldn't be scorpions hiding in my tent when I got back. *Duct tape! That's it—duct tape!*

I went inside my tent, pulled out a roll of duct tape, and tore off a piece. I put it over the small gap where the horizontal and vertical zippers met. Then I tossed the duct tape on the ground near the base of the tent and started to walk away, only to stop again. *What if a scorpion or even a snake crawls under or near the duct tape, and when I go to pick it up next time* . . .

I turned around, aggravated. *What a freakin' hassle!*

I picked up the duct tape, put it on the roof of the tent, and told myself I would inspect it before I reached for it next time—because, as my friend Dmitri had told me, "scorpions can climb." Actually, he had given me this bit of information after I came up with the idea of bringing a cot to the desert.

"The cot will get me off the ground," I said excitedly, "and make it more difficult for scorpions to . . ."

"Won't work," Dmitri said. "They'll just climb up the inside wall of your tent and onto the ceiling, then drop onto you while you're asleep . . ."

"Well, at least the nasty little critters have to get in first," I muttered to myself as I started off in the direction of the cave once again.

The one and only time I had seen the cave was with Tamir just a few days before. He had taken me to the first of the three sites he recommended for my forty days in the desert. I didn't remember too much about the cave and its surroundings other than that it was rocky. I was so freaked out by the "newness" of everything in the desert that everything blurred together. That's why I was afraid even to walk very far from my tent—because every place in the desert looked the same. At least to me, because everything was just sand and rock—and the only difference from one place to the next was the size of the rocks and the amount of sand.

There were only two landmarks I could pick out in the desert.

One was the Dead Sea. It·was only two miles away, so any time I saw a body of water fifty miles long, I at least knew that was the Dead Sea. But even a fifty-mile body of water could easily disappear behind any one of a number of small brown hills once you climbed over them. And if you got yourself turned around the wrong way—even with a compass—who knew what could happen?

The other recognizable marker in the desert was something I had seen just that morning while having a cup of coffee with Ya'el back at the hostel. As we sat outside, I pointed to a dark figure a mile or two away. It was up on one of the countless desert hills.

"Is that a person?" I asked.

"No," she answered, "it's a statue, a memorial commemorating all the people who died in that canyon."

"Are there many people who die out there?" I asked while

thinking about the chances of my own name winding up on that memorial.

"Oh yes," she said, "every year there are a few."

So while I walked toward the cave, which was between my tent and the Dead Sea, I kept looking back toward my tent to make sure I had a sense of where I was coming from and where I was going.

When I finally found the cave, I was surprised at how barren it was. There was nothing in it except more rocks, sand, and, well, I guess there was something new—a whole bunch of pigeon crap. I was concerned at first, because I remembered reading somewhere about the health hazards of inhaling it—but then again, it was 125 degrees outside, and I had no other place to go. So I tentatively sat down in the cave and wiped the dust and dry, chalky pigeon droppings from my hands.

The cave was actually more of a stone veranda than a cave, and it was millions of years old.

"The cave, like everything else in this canyon, is limestone," Tamir had said.

"The limestone is probably thirty to seventy million years old, and it was formed from the lime of shells from aquatic life compacted by the weight of the deep sea. This canyon is a young canyon compared to the bigger canyons in Israel. It's been formed over the last twenty-five million years."

The only wall in the cave was part of a cliff face, which I kept at my back. The cliff overhang jutted out over me and was supported by a stone pillar that was about eight feet from the wall and ten feet in circumference.

In movies, caves always have soft, sandy floors, but this cave's floor was made up of boulders. I sat cross-legged on the uneven stone floor. My butt and legs hurt as bone pressed against rock. I tried lying down, but there wasn't one flat place in the whole cave where a rock wasn't sticking squarely in the middle of my back. It was so hot that I could barely breathe. It was a sauna, but without a door by which to leave. As I lay there, my body tightened, my eyes bugged out, and I realized, *I am more uncomfortable than I have ever been in my life . . . and there's no way to make it better.*

But then I was suddenly distracted. The ceiling was *moving.*

"What the . . . ?"

Some kind of lizard, with bloodshot eyes that bugged out almost as much as mine, was crawling along the ceiling. It stopped and looked at me. Its eyes were locked on mine. *Is it trying to stare me down? Should I keep looking back at it? Don't they always say you shouldn't stare into the eyes of wild animals? That you'll spook them or something, and they'll attack?*

Then it dawned on me that I wore tan desert clothing, the same color as the cave. Maybe the lizard thought I was just another rock, and it was getting ready to jump down on me, perhaps grabbing my throat and biting me.

Do they have teeth?

I rolled onto my side, giving the lizard a more difficult angle of attack. I calculated my chances of swatting it away in midair in case it leaped in my direction. After watching each other, both of us motionless for a good forty minutes, the lizard moved away, its butt and tail swaying like Chubby Checker doing the twist.

I lay there for hours that seemed like weeks.

After sundown, I walked back to my tent and sprawled out on the foam mat. The wind picked up so strongly that the front half of the tent rose a foot off the ground whenever it blew. I piled a couple of duffel bags by the door in an attempt to weight down the base, but that only increased the size of my billowing tent until I thought it would rip open at the seams.

There's only one way to deal with this problem, I decided.

I sat up, grabbed a bag of pistachios, and ate them nervously, so quickly that I became a machine, barely having cracked one open and placed it in my mouth before I was already onto the next nut. Cracking and chewing, cracking and chewing. Before I knew it, I had eaten almost a pound of nuts. Then I ate some dried apricots, a Clif Bar, and some more dried fruit. Any awareness of a potential disaster had been partly numbed by my eating, but eventually I was full and once again at the mercy of the wind and my anxiety.

Sweating profusely, I lay back down on the foam mat. Then I was overcome by the all-pervading sense that I wasn't going to be allowed out of the desert alive. *I could die here.* That's why I had made out a will before I came. When I told my friend Roger where I kept it, he just sighed and looked like he was going to cry. Roger didn't have a lot of close friends, and we had lost one mutual best friend in the past year, so the thought of losing the other was almost too much for him to bear.

"Please, God," I prayed, "help me right now. Please don't let the tent rip open. I'm kind of really scared . . . please help me with my fear . . ."

I continued praying this way for I don't know how long, until, somehow, I fell asleep.

day 2

I dreamed last night that Chokyi Nyima, a Tibetan lama I know, said he would call me while I was in the desert to see how I was doing. I awoke remembering his smiling face. Some people would question whether it was really the lama coming into my dream or just my own mind creating him. Either way, all I know is that when I see Chokyi Nyima's face in my mind's eye and allow it to dissolve, the joyful nurturance that was his face becomes a joyful nurturance that is me. The same thing has often happened with Jesus. Whenever I see his loving presence within me and allow it to dissolve, it becomes my loving presence, and perhaps even more accurate, our loving presence.

It was so hard this morning. I woke up early and explored the canyon, looking for a more comfortable place than the cave in which to spend the day, but I could go out in the sun for only fifteen or twenty minutes at a time before I had to retreat and find shade. Even then, the shady spots were there one moment and gone the next as the sun moved across the sky. I moved around like a homeless person, every hour or two kicked out of my temporary shelter.

The intense heat of the sun made the choice clear; actually, I had no choice—it was either the cave or go home. But I didn't like the cave. It gave me the creeps; there were so many cracks and crevices where scorpions and snakes might be hiding.

Plus, the floor was a series of undulating limestone boulders—it felt as if I were lying on a bed of shoes, only the shoes were rocks that couldn't be moved. At other times, I felt as though I were lying across a miniature mountain range and had to make my body into Jell-O—soft and flexible—so that I could lie with my legs over one mountain peak while the small of my back relaxed into an adjacent valley before my midback, neck, and head hit the upslope of the next mountain.

Despite that discomfort, I began to feel better about the cave. I had been inside for just fifteen minutes—and what a difference! It was unbearably hot only five feet from me in the sun, but in this cave it wasn't too bad.

Then I saw my first mouse. He was so fat that he looked like a furry brown tennis ball with legs and a tail. He sniffed around under a ledge next to my cave until he realized I was there— then he was gone. I also saw a lot of lizards. I lay on my back and watched them crawl across the cave walls and ceiling. The lizards came in various colors; some were brown, almost black, and others were stone/sand-colored lizards that were hard to see because they blended in with rocks of the same color. One salamander seemed to be gobbling something up every inch or so, perhaps insects so small I couldn't see them. I was able to watch the salamander above me without any concern for a sneak attack because I was wearing my mosquito hat with the net down over my face.

The desert changes so much in twenty-four hours. During the day, the intense heat is oppressive and brutal, and the insects and birds keep up a constant chatter. But then dusk comes, and when I emerge from the cave and climb the rocky cliffs up to the plateau, I step into a different world. With sunset come the beautiful pastel pinks, purples, and blues—a backdrop to the overlapping, gently rolling hills and flat wide-open spaces. The landscape looks like a herd of giant whales, each having surfaced and in the midst of submerging again; only their great brown-and-tan humped backs are visible.

The desert seems alive even as it is dead. The cliffs and stones have a sentient character, as an elderly Navajo would have; their ancient wisdom shaped, colored, and lined by the sun and the wind. Even the sand seems to have a soul, and, actually, the word *sand* is misleading because the ground isn't sandy—it's hard, stony, and brittle. It even refused my attempts at staking my tent by cracking and breaking into small pieces and fragments until I felt like an incompetent sculptor; chipping away at a desert that would never take my shape.

They say the Essenes, members of one of the major sects of Judaism at the time of Jesus, lived in this area. I can see how this would have been possible. The rocks and boulders seem to have been thrown across the cliffs and hillsides, dumped on top of one another from some cosmic sack, every once in a while one falling against another just so, forming a small pocket (in which birds made their home) or perhaps something larger, such as a cave. The Essenes lived in these caves, and it was in places like these that they hid their religious books, what have come to be known as the Dead Sea Scrolls, from the onslaught of the Roman Empire.

Some speculate that Jesus or John studied with the Essenes and learned about baptism and repentance from them. Others also suggest that John the Baptist was probably Jesus's teacher for a while. Eventually Jesus even went beyond John, to his lonesome, individual adventure out in the desert.

That's why I've come to the desert: to go beyond what I've been taught.

AFTERNOON

"Ow!" I said out loud after I stood up too high in the cave and solid rock met my not-so-solid head.

I rubbed my head furiously, trying to concentrate on the rubbing more than the pain. They should make a hat for idiots like me that reads "Duck your head, mate; the cave is about to pound you one on the noggin."

Tamir or Ya'el will bring me a mosquito net in a few days. In his original e-mails to me, Tamir said that "water, shade, and a mosquito net or mosquito hat" were most important in the desert. I'll also ask them to bring instant coffee and a few more mats. It appears that I will be living in this cave, at least during the day, which means I will spend the hours from 7:00 a.m. to 7:00 p.m. here—and a few more mats on the rocky floor will make it bearable.

The site where I'm staying now is the first and only place Tamir took me. He had planned on taking me to three sites and giving me a choice, but he began complaining about soreness in his ear (which later turned out to be a punctured eardrum). Still, for a day, he toughed it out as he showed me the desert he loves.

"See how the rock is as white as the moon," he said; "that's from all the limestone and the sun bleaching it.

"See that house in the middle of nowhere," he said, pointing as we came around a bend; "that's the little house on the prairie—and we Israelis named it that way before the television show."

Then Tamir pulled the car over to the side of the road and reached across the passenger seat and out the window, tearing some leaves from a shrub.

"This is the maluach bush," he said, handing me a powdery-looking green leaf. "Taste this."

I bit off a piece. "This is really salty," I said.

"If you fry it in some olive oil," he added, "it tastes just like potato chips."

"Look over there," Tamir said, pointing to a black bird flapping its wings in the middle of the road. "Birds of prey stand out in the sun and spread their wings. The fleas get too hot—and they leave. So if you get ants in your black duffel bags, just put them out in the sun, and the heat will kill the ants or they will crawl away."

But the descent from Jerusalem (2,700 feet above sea level) to the Dead Sea, the lowest point on earth (almost 1,400 feet below sea level), eventually got to Tamir.

"Bill," Tamir said as he rested on a stone ledge, "I am very sorry, but something's wrong with my ear."

I was lying on the same stone ledge as Tamir. The ledge was part of a dry riverbed that ran down to the edge of a cliff. Actually, we were lying in what only a few months earlier had been a rushing, gushing waterfall. Just above us on the plateau, three wadis met and flowed into one another, and the flow of that water, though present for only a few hours two or three times a year, had managed over the last twenty-five million years to carve a canyon through the limestone.

After the first night on the open plateau, when I thought my tent was going to be ripped open by the wind and blown away, I decided to pitch it in one of the dry wadis up on the plateau. The tent now fit snugly between the wadi's walls, and several bushes were tucked along the sides. I had heard stories about people who had pitched their tents in dry riverbeds, only to be killed by flash floods. But Tamir had assured me there was no danger of that. "There is no chance of rain," Tamir said. "If it rained it would be local, and you would have thirty minutes to get out. If you didn't, the worst that would happen this time of year is that your things would be floating in thirty centimeters—about a foot—of water."

Tamir was a godsend to me. For the past couple of years, I had looked for a way to spend forty days in the Judean desert, but every overture or attempt I made was met with skepticism (read: people thought I was crazy), unanswered e-mails, or letters that flat out said, "No way."

It was a couple of years ago that I first decided to go into the desert as Jesus had. My next decision was where—which desert? The answer to that was easy enough, because I wanted to go where Jesus had spent his time in the desert. But that was where things got more difficult, because the Bible does not specify which desert Jesus went to.

Legend has it that Jesus stayed at a place in Israel now called the Mount of Temptation. So my initial plan was to stay there, perhaps in the caves that hermits had occupied in the twelfth and thirteenth centuries, or in the Greek Orthodox monastery that had been built there. I wrote to the Greek patriarch, asking permission to stay at the monastery. I received a letter denying my request, saying that they did not have adequate facilities for an extended visit of forty days, and sending their prayers for my "fruitful visit of contemplation."

I was frustrated when I was denied my forty days and nights at the monastery. But in hindsight I was glad, because I discovered that the Mount of Temptation had changed since Jesus's time. Tens of millions of dollars had been invested there. A Swiss-Australian-built cable car now took tourists the three hundred meters up to the monastery, and the trip took five minutes instead of thirty. They also built a casino with a golf course, tennis courts, and a five-star Sheraton Hotel. There were also two new French-Oriental restaurants. Can you imagine the new twist the devil would have had in his temptations of Jesus? Instead of tempting Jesus to "turn this stone into bread," it would be "Hey, I'll run next door and get you some egg foo yong. Whaddya think?"

I read that the three monks who lived at the monastery were in a frenzy because after a century of solitude, they expected five hundred thousand tourists this year. Even the Greek patriarch must have been thinking about business, because he had the monks extend their open hours from 8:00 a.m. to 7:00 p.m.

The Mount of Temptation had gone Las Vegas. The solitude and barren simplicity that Jesus had sought were gone. I imagined staying at the Sheraton Hotel for forty days and writing about how in the midst of luxury, a human being can still feel as empty and as desolate as in a desert—perhaps even more so—but that thought lasted only a moment.

Then the Israelis and Palestinians started killing one another again, so my trip to Israel became too dangerous. It would be hard enough battling my own fears and demons in the Judean desert, and I didn't need the added fears and paranoia of being taken hostage by a Palestinian terrorist group or being shot by an Israeli soldier. Yet I didn't want to give up on the idea of being in the same desert, the same environment, that Jesus had stayed in for forty days.

What could I do?

That's when I looked at a map of the Middle East and noticed that the Jordan River (where Jesus was baptized by John the Baptist just before he went into the desert) was on the border between Israel and Jordan. Did Jesus spend time in Jordan? After some more research, I found that Jesus had traveled to the region of Judea that was east of the Jordan and spent time healing and preaching to people in the Jordanian towns of Bethany, Decapolis, and Gadara.

Furthermore, I discovered that some modern archaeologists believe Jesus was baptized on the east side of the Jordan River—the Jordan side. If this was true, then it made sense that after Jesus emerged from the east side of the Jordan River and heard the voice from heaven say, "You are my Son, whom I love; with you I am well pleased," and was immediately sent into the desert by the Spirit, he may have gone east into the Jordanian desert. But I received no replies after numerous e-mails to various Jordanian organizations, so I was back at square one.

Then, after a year of trying every idea I could think of without success, my friend Bonnie suggested I call Rabbi Zalman Schachter. Rabbi Zalman gave me the phone number of Rabbi

Ohad in Israel, who then gave me the phone number of a Judean desert guide named Tamir.

"Yes, I have just the place for you," Tamir said when I called him. "It's in the Judean desert, near Qumran, Ein Gedi, and the Dead Sea. No one goes there, and you will be safe."

Tamir was thirty-seven years old, an ex–Israeli intelligence officer who loved the desert. When I arrived in Jerusalem, I saw that even his apartment was like a desert. It was sparse like the desert, but with cushions on the floors instead of rocks. And just like in the desert, Tamir let the bugs freely come and go. He thought they belonged there as much as he did.

"Ouch!" he said while washing dishes at his house during my first night in Jerusalem.

"I stepped on a bumblebee," he explained, bending down and sliding the insect onto a piece of paper. "That was the second time this week."

Then, instead of just tossing the bee outside, Tamir looked at it closely while it died. He studied it the way a jeweler studies gems—only with more empathy for his subject.

Tamir lived simply. He was efficient and hated to waste anything. He ate only natural foods, which were kept in old peanut butter jars on unpainted shelves. One day I showed him my water purifier, which was advertised as "the water purifier of the U.S. Marine Corps," and in one end of which I supposedly could dump muddy water and hand-pump clear water out the other. Tamir said, "Here's mine," and held up two plastic water bottles with the bottoms cut off and turned upside down. They were tied together, and inside them were layers of soil, crushed stone, and sand.

"I can get a liter of purified water a night with this," he said proudly.

Speaking of purifiers, what is the deal with this Jesus-dying-for-our-sins stuff? Somehow his death purified me and got rid of my sins? I have thirty-nine more days and nights to ponder that one.

I brought five books with me into the desert—my last book, *A Place at the Table*; and four translations of the Bible, because different translations make subtle but huge differences. For example, when David talks to God in Psalm 139:8, the New International Version says, "If I go up to the heavens, you are there; if I make my bed *in the depths*, you are there" (emphasis added), while the King James Version says, "If I ascend up into heaven, thou art there: if I make my bed *in hell*, behold, thou art there" (emphasis added).

I brought the King James Version, the New International Version, the New American Standard Bible, and *The Five Gospels* by the Jesus Seminar, which contains the four Gospels of the New Testament along with the Gospel of Thomas, in which, among many other things, Jesus says, "If you bring forth what is within you, what you have will save you" (page 53, vs.70).

DUSK

Now that the sun is down, I feel very happy, and tears come to my eyes. I must admit, I was worried there for a while this morning. It was unbearably hot. Too hot to pray, meditate, write, or relax. It was just survival; a resistance of the elements by my body, and a resistance of my body by my spirit. The body doesn't like discomfort, and neither does the spirit. That's why I had to focus on inhabiting my body with my spirit when things became difficult.

MIDDLE OF THE NIGHT

I moved my tent twice today before deciding on a spot in a wadi. The tent is partially protected from strong winds by the banks of the wadi, which rise up eight to ten feet on both sides. So while I have the wind problem somewhat solved, the biggest problem is that during the day the ground absorbs all the heat; so even after the sun goes down, I lie here in my tent, and it's as though I'm lying on top of a stove. I tried laying down two quarter-inch foam mats with a sleeping bag on top, but it didn't help. I just lay there, naked and sweating. Finally, I couldn't stand it any longer, so I grabbed two duffel bags, stuffed them with clothes and gear, and then lay sprawled across the top of them. But there was no way I could sleep that way, and it was so uncomfortable that it wasn't long before I was back on the ground. This went on for hours. Overtired and anxious, I felt my ability to tolerate the situation wearing thin. I ate the rest of the pistachio nuts and finally fell asleep sometime in the early morning—exhausted.

day 3

I slept late this morning, trying to recover from my desert-induced exhaustion. A pain in my stomach finally woke me up. After drinking some water, I started to cramp. The pain was like a knife in my belly, and as I stumbled out of the tent, all I could think of was getting rid of it.

And now that I had to go to the bathroom for the first time since coming to the desert, I wondered, *Where? Where should I go?* Tamir had said not to do this too close to my tent because the flies would land on it, then fly over to me or my food and contaminate my food. But a few steps away from my tent, my belly cramped up more, and then I felt dizzy, and then . . .

The next thing I knew, I was pushing my face into broken glass. *Why am I pushing my face into broken glass?* I asked myself. Then I slowly opened my eyes, and I didn't know where I was or what I was doing. I felt the weight of my face on something. It wasn't one object; it was many small ones—irregularly shaped and pointed. *I'm lying facedown in a pile of rocks.* I pressed against the ground with my hands and slowly raised myself up while spitting out pieces of stone and wiping away the last bits that still clung to my face.

I had passed out.

The cramping started again, so I staggered over to the nearest rock, pulled down my pants, and sat down. It was too close to my tent, but I didn't care because I was so nauseated and shaky that I would have defecated in my back pocket if it would have helped.

Flies and mosquitoes attacked. For a moment I thought I'd vomit. I shivered as chills and goose bumps ran up and down my body. *How can I be shivering when it's 100 degrees out?* I felt something on my forehead and reached up to touch it. I looked at my fingers.

Blood?

I touched my hand to my forehead and looked again—more blood.

Oh, God—I'm bleeding.

My jaw tightened while I stared at the blood.

"This is when the journey really starts," I said.

I shooed away the flies and mosquitoes, then gingerly felt the gash on my forehead, trying to assess how severe it was. I looked at the blood a third time and then felt a wave of nausea and cramping so intense that I actually wanted my mommy. Everything seemed to close in on me—the heat, the bugs, the pain and sickness, and especially the fear that I might die. I was overwhelmed. I wanted to retreat from the discomfort, to curl up in a ball and die, but something in me wouldn't allow me to give up. Instead, I realized I needed to cry, so I buried my head in my hands and wept—releasing such a deep, paralyzing tension and fear that I was surprised to find I hadn't sweat blood in the process.

While crying, I became aware that no one was coming (or would come) to comfort or take care of me. After I felt I had cried enough, I accepted the fact that I had to pull myself together—the irony being that my first step toward doing that was something as basic as having to wipe myself.

I then struggled to my feet and walked to my tent in a sort of low crouch so that if I passed out again, I wouldn't have as far to fall. And maybe if I felt dizzy, I could even sit down before I passed out. I didn't want to wake up facedown on a pile of rocks for the second time this morning. I might not wake up next time, and there wasn't another human being within miles of here to save me from baking in the 130-degree midday heat.

Inside the tent, I pulled a mirror out of my duffel bag. It was cracked and fell in pieces onto the ground. I picked up a piece and looked at myself

"Oh, God!" I said.

My forehead was gashed wide open. The cramping and dizziness returned. I put the mirror down. The blood ran down my forehead. It was so hot—so incredibly hot, and it was only seven in the morning.

I got out my first-aid kit.

"Scrub the laceration," the directions read.

After I finished scrubbing with an iodine pad, I pinched together the edges of the laceration and taped it closed with two butterfly bandages. *Will it get infected? Do I need stitches?* I hoped the scar wouldn't look too ghastly. For a moment I imagined my grandson sitting on my knee.

"Grandpa," he asked, "how did you get that boo-boo?"

"Well, son," I began, "I was in the Judean desert thirty years ago—that's where Jesus was, you know, and . . ."

And it was on this third day in the Judean desert that I first began to bleed—and then die, over and over again.

That's it. I've had it. The flies are making me crazy! I'm in my cave, and even though I'm covered by clothes and a mosquito hat, they're crawling and buzzing only millimeters from my face and ears, and they are pushing me over the edge! Since I have the hat on, I'm hotter and I sweat more; consequently, the perspiration on my forehead is causing the bandages not to adhere as well, and the wound keeps opening up. If I remove the hat in an attempt to cool off, the flies keep landing on my wounds.

I can identify with my friend Dave, who felt these same tortures. But instead of flies attacking him, it was his own thoughts. He had no hope of relieving himself of them. Me? I'm here for only forty days; then it's good-bye, bugs. Anyway, Tamir is supposed to bring a mosquito net on Monday. That should make the cave quite luxurious.

Large wasps and birds increasingly come near my cave. It turns out there is a small hole, about the size of a pitcher of beer, next to the cave. At the bottom the sand is wet, and there are a few tablespoons of water. The bugs and birds are all stopping there for a drink.

I fantasize that a pool of water is forming and eventually a spring will erupt. And then, after I leave, people will forever come to *my* cave and see the miracle of "the spontaneous pool and spring."

"This is where the great saint lived for forty days," they'll say. I catch myself thinking this way and quietly leave that part of my mind alone. Grandiose thoughts will not help or comfort me here. Doing what needs to be done and just "being" are the things that comfort me here; add a cup of coffee and some creating, and I'm fulfilled—at least for now.

I asked Jesus for healing. If my wound gets infected, I might have to leave.

"I know there are some things I should ask for and some things I shouldn't," I said. "Please help heal my body; I don't want to leave."

"Why?" he asked.

"Well, it would be a little embarrassing—but more than that, I really wanted to be here for forty days."

"Why?"

"You were here!"

"I'm everywhere."

"But I felt called to come here."

"Was it me who called you, or you?"

NIGHT

I changed my dressing for the third time today and then lay down.

I can't do this! It's too hard. It's too hot—and to make matters worse, the flies sent out word to all the other flies that I'm here.

When I tried to cook, they were on me. When I put antibiotic on my forehead, they were on me. And when I tried to sleep in the cave, they were on me! At times, there were upward of ten to fifteen flies at a time.

Even though I had the mosquito-net hat, it was still incredibly annoying because the flies crawled all over me and made me feel like a fresh pile of dung. I was forced to lie there covered head to toe, wearing a long-sleeved shirt and long pants, with my hands folded beneath a second hat I placed on my belly. Still they crawled all over me, looking for an entrance to what? What was I to them? Food? Some kind of game to help them pass the time?

I must have looked like Dave as he lay in bed motionless—not wanting to react to the presence of any other living thing. But with one very important difference. I had faith, and because of that I opened my body to the presence of Spirit as I lay there and tried not to grasp at my reactions. Dave numbed his body, allowing the gravity of his dark self to press down upon him. For most of Dave's life his strategy had been to retreat from darkness through cleverness, until one day when he retreated into a corner and there was nowhere to go as the darkness closed in. The same cleverness that had defended him up until then now turned against him, creating fears that drove him into mental illness. The only way out, as far as he could see, was death.

That was my way out, too, or perhaps I should say, my way through and back. The irony of it all was that twenty years ago, it was Dave who had found *my* diary and *my* suicide notes.

"Bill," he had said, tossing my black-covered notebook at me, "are you planning to kill yourself?"

Why did I live and Dave die? Was I a better person? A more clever person? A more spiritual person? Perhaps the most important question was, why was I given faith, when Dave was not?

This question of faith, or the lack thereof, is partly what killed Dave. Because the main difference I see between Dave and me is that Dave *coped* with his darkness while I *worked through* my darkness and fear. I went into my darkness, through penetrating meditation retreats of ten days in silence and years of therapy, because I had been given a faith that accompanied me into the darkness.

But Dave meditated in ways that only coped with darkness and fear. He meditated to relax and feel good—when he wanted to. When the difficult places arose in meditation, he got up and did something else. That's why I did a ten-day retreat at least once a year. I had to sit there—even when I didn't want to, which is often the most productive time. Even our therapists were different. Dave picked a therapist whom he was smarter than, and he always kept the therapist at a distance. But my therapists pushed me, and though I hate to admit it, they sometimes knew more than I did.

Was it faith that allowed me to be with the fear and go deeper, while Dave—lacking faith—had no choice but to protect himself by avoiding his fear and his depth? Was that it? Did it come down to faith? And where did this faith come from? The kind of faith that tells me, "No matter what happens to me—I am loved."

It's so hot; I can't pray, meditate, or do yoga. I don't even want to read or write. I'm just surviving tonight. But I want to do more than that. I want to relax into my environment, interact with it and let it in; to be like water and flow into its cracks; to enter it as it enters me.

But that's not happening, I'm only surviving in this place. I feel stuck here, and resisting my surroundings won't allow me to be at home here. I want to feel the desert in me and not just resist it.

I lay in my tent—naked; the only thing covering me is sweat. Why am I sweating in my tent at eight thirty at night? I thought about the many ways I could leave. How embarrassing. I told *everyone* I'd be here forty days. Just the thought of returning after three or four days is humbling. If I quit now, would I quit easily on everything after this? Oh, God, I'm not going to make it! I'm scared because my mind and body are feeling odd. I'm tired—yet it's more than tired—*I'm exhausted*. Am I heat-exhausted? Am I sick and sinking into a confused delirium? Do people even know when they're getting delirious? Will they have to lift me out with a helicopter? Who would pay? I don't have health insurance. Not that I would be covered in another country anyway. When I was sick in England in 1980, England's national health insurance paid. *They paid for me!* But I'm not in England—I'm in Israel.

As I lay in my tent sweating, I felt like an ice cube melting in the midday heat. Eventually nothing would be left of me. *Am I going to die? Am I dying right now and don't even realize it?* Perhaps I'd end up like James Pike, the Episcopal bishop who went out into the Judean desert in 1969 and died of dehydration. I am afraid to stay, but I am also afraid to leave. I don't want to die in the desert, and I certainly don't want to die because of my own stubbornness.

Again and again, I try to see myself objectively. *Is the smart thing to leave now before I get even sicker? Or is my own fear just scaring me into going home?* I can't tell.

I began to pray.

"Dear God, Jesus, I need your help. I want to stay, but I don't know if I can. I'm a very stubborn man, so I need your help. Please make it plain to me if I need to leave, because I don't want to die out here . . ."

My mind continued to spiral, driven by ever-increasing fear and doubt. I continued asking God for direction and waiting for an answer. The beginning of the answer came when I realized I had to pee. I stood up, grabbed a flashlight, and stepped out of the tent—naked, except for my sandals. I was met by the desert wind moving across my body, blessing me with its cool, angelic touch. I felt immediate relief.

While urinating out on the plateau, I scoured the countryside for wild animals. Then I looked up at the immense night sky with its bright lights high in the darkness—and for the first time in my life, I realized that the night was alive—deep, vibrant, and pregnant.

What must the ancients have thought? If I were an ancient, I would have thought the stars to be pinholes in the dark fabric that covered the sky. The sun must be behind that black fabric, still shining, but only through pinholes.

I stood there, letting go into the awe-inspiring darkness until I no longer felt alone.

I breathed deeply, my body and being coming alive, renewed and refreshed. If the whole day was like this, I could do it! In my tent only moments before, I was hot, sweaty, thinking of ways out—but now, standing naked under the heavens, I was rejuvenated and reminded that I wasn't alone. *Maybe I can make it . . .*

day 4

I'm learning that the desert has rules.

The first rule is, you can't be stupid in the desert.

If the desert asks something from you and you don't do it, you will get hurt or die. I had overdone it the first few days when I put up my tent three times in three different places, carried hundreds of pounds of supplies, and ate too many nuts and too much dried fruit. I was stupid, and so I got hurt.

The second rule is, respect the desert.

I learned that I had to constantly assess my relationship to the desert. *Respect* comes from the Latin and means "to look again," and I had to constantly look again: first at the desert, then at myself, then at our relationship. I respected the desert; I looked at her, felt her, then softened my edges to fit into her landscape. There were beginning to be moments when I relaxed, which meant I relaxed everything I believed myself to be and then felt the desert and myself blending together. I manipulated the desert when I could, by moving a rock here or there, but for the most part I allowed the desert to direct my life, and I lived within the life the desert gave me.

Since my anger, frustration (a constant), and tantrums (another constant) did not change the desert, I began changing myself. I relaxed my hold on my thoughts till they were more landscape, like the birds flying here or there. When emotions welled up, I did not feed them with more reactivity. Instead, I relaxed my grasping at them, and they lessened until they eventually left.

I learned that emotions move slowly, unlike thoughts, which darted about in my mind like the flies in my cave. I watched my emotions coming and then watched them move through, over, and away from me like one of those ants that slowly walked across my body as I lay in my cave.

I am developing a slight rhythm. I'm learning desert ways and desert hours—not my way. Don't get me wrong; I do things my way when I can, but in the end, the desert decides.

For example, when do I cook? Do I cook when it's hot out? Or do I cook before the sun comes up and after it goes down? When do I drink water? All the time! Especially when I think I don't need to, like during the night when I'm sleeping. If I sleep eight hours and don't drink water—that's eight hours in the desert without water. Not good!

When do I get up? I thought I could sleep till 6:30 or 7:00 a.m. But if I do that, then as I cook breakfast or make coffee or get my gear together, I'll be sweating heavily in the heat. Then by the time I make it to my cave, I'll be drenched in sweat and hot. I learned to get up early, say 4:30 to 5:00 a.m., when it's cool, allowing me to take my time getting ready without sweating too much. Whoever wrote that book *Don't Sweat the Small Stuff* never lived in the desert!

Take my time. I'm learning how to do that. Sometimes it's so hot that I hurriedly try to finish what I'm doing so I can get into the shade. But hurrying heats up my body and mind even more. I've learned that anxiety has a certain heat to it. It heats the body, which then may easily bubble up into anger, and I'm sure this kind of anxiety and the psyche-mind-body heat it produces result in many illnesses.

So I take my time—what's the hurry? More important, I don't leave things to the last moment; otherwise, I suffer.

B. F. Skinner was right about conditioned responses, because in some ways I'm just a pigeon pecking at a button. If I peck the right button, I'm not hot, I'm not sweating, and I'm not collapsing onto a pile of rocks and stones. I can even relax and enjoy. But if I fail to press the right button for whatever reason . . . *bzzz!* Penalty on Bill Elliott! For example, if I'm lazy and don't prepare properly before it gets hot . . . *bzzz!* Penalty on Bill Elliott! He will sweat uncomfortably for twenty minutes!

Or *bzzz!* Penalty on Bill Elliott. He left his tent open because of inattention. There are now flies buzzing around his head as he lies down and mosquitoes looking for the best place to strike.

And again, *bzzz!* Penalty on Bill Elliott. He tried to do two things at once. He was climbing down the cliff and thinking about something else. He slipped, banged a knee, skinned his buttock, and now feels the fear of making a similar mistake that could result in his death.

I hear my friend Dave say, "You're getting it, Wonder Brother; you're getting it." Dave loved the outdoors. He was more himself, at least the self he felt comfortable being, when he was outdoors. The outdoors is probably what sustained him for forty-three years before he committed suicide. I have a lot of his gear on my trip. His backpack, duffel bag, water bottle, pocketknife, and sleeping bag.

For a while I didn't want to take his stuff. Perhaps it was haunted and had dark, depressed "Dave energy" in it—the energy that he wallowed in the last year or so till he killed himself.

I even have his duct tape. The tape he used to connect the hose to the exhaust pipe on his car, just before he killed himself on May 4, 2000. Actually, I don't have *the* tape; that would be too creepy. But I have one of the extra rolls he had lying around.

Dave had duct tape everywhere—on old shoes, on sleeping bags (I swear half his sleeping bag is duct tape), on his rain poncho, and also on some weird contraption he made in which duct tape connects an orange juice can to a fist-sized glass orb. Inside is a needle balanced on a small pin. Maybe it's a compass? I never thought of that. Or a barometer? Or just something that moves whenever a friendly spirit is in the room?

Dave was intensely fun, partly because he was creative, a visionary. He was Creative with a big *C*. Dave *saw*, if you know what I mean. He would see a situation or a happening and give it a name, a label that had never existed before.

"If Webster can do it," Dave said, "why can't I?"

He called bike riding "falling into the future" because "you're leaning forward as though you're falling while propelling yourself forward with your legs—into the future." And whenever he stumbled, tripped over a crack, or dropped something, he'd say, "Bad gravity."

I guess the last year of Dave's life—when he was just lying in bed, almost comatose, like a man whose body had died and whose only sign of life was in his eyes—was one whole year of "bad gravity" for Dave. Toward the end, he didn't even move his head to acknowledge you while he lay in bed; instead, he just moved his eyes toward or away from you. Yeah, definitely, that final year for Dave was bad gravity. He had fallen, and fallen, and fallen. One fall led to another; one stumble or fall set in motion the next. I wonder, *Now that he's dead, is he still falling?*

LATE MORNING

I'm in my cave. I heard a strange sound. Is it a bird? Or is it Tamir and Ya'el, visiting and calling to me? I'm not budging from my cave to look for them. It's too hot out there. They'll have to find me if they're here.

It's been a couple of days since I bumped my head. I always look up now before I stand. I hope that lesson does not have to be reinforced.

Hey, who knows, if I were staying longer, I would probably take a pad and duct-tape it to my ceiling. Like I said, the desert always has her way, but if her edges can sometimes be softened a bit, there's no reason to suffer unnecessarily. Probably the wisest saying ever (especially when applied to the desert) is the serenity prayer by Reinhold Niebuhr: "God, give us grace to accept with serenity the things that cannot be changed, courage to change the things which should be changed, and the wisdom to distinguish the one from the other."

Besides the flies, mosquitoes, and ants, I have a few other residents in my cave. Actually, I don't think the bugs live here in the cave. They just work here and then bring home the fruits of their labor. Sort of like people who live in New Jersey and work in New York; they drive across the bridge, do their eight-hour stint, and go home again.

I've met a few lizards. The first day I saw one or two scamper away from me. But now I just lie on the stone floor of the cave and watch them move along the walls and ceilings. They're about eight inches long and tan colored; they blend in with the stone. If I didn't see them move, I probably would miss them. Their feet have little suction cups on the toes. They move very quickly along the walls and ceiling. I haven't seen one fall yet.

Occasionally birds fly in and out of my cave. There's a ton of bird droppings in there. Is this one of their resting places? They fly in quietly and then out. I wonder if they eat bugs. In that case, I'd wish they'd visit me more often.

It became quite clear today that Jesus was not alone for forty days. He was a man, with a man's body, and even if you think he was God incarnate, he still had a body and must have needed shade and a source of water. He probably wouldn't have materialized any water or food for himself as he did with the loaves and fish to feed the five thousand, because Jesus never did a miracle for himself; it was always for other people.

While he could have found shade in different solitary places, freshwater came from springs or wells, and those were public places. He probably met other human beings while wandering near water holes. I'm drinking almost two gallons of water a day, and since a gallon weighs almost eight and a half pounds, Jesus couldn't have carried much water or traveled very far from a water source. One Christian monk told me that he thought Jesus stayed on the outskirts of the city and went more deeply into the desert only for brief times. I'm only several miles from the hostel, and yet I'm far enough away to be as good as dead if I do something stupid. What I'm saying is, there's no one out here to help or hinder me. After my "passing out" episode, I'm leery of walking too near the cliffs. If I faint there, it's "bye-bye, Bill."

I fainted once before like that. So I know there are warnings and unique circumstances involved. A few years ago I was golfing on a terribly hot day after eating a lot of pizza the night before. The cheese and all the salt in the pizza caused me to sweat profusely. On the twelfth hole, a tough 170-yard par 3, I was lining up a forty-five-foot putt for a birdie when I suddenly got a stomach cramp and passed out next to the green. Waking up almost immediately, I told my golf partners that I was lagging up and then going to the bathroom.

"Just give me the second putt," I said.

Immediately after I stroked the ball, I started a trot to the outhouse. Halfway there, I could hear them yell. I turned to see the ball dropping into the cup for a deuce (that day I shot a 74). I had the same cramping then as I did yesterday, so any future cramping will be a warning. Like yesterday, that golf day was hot. Combine that with my usual low blood pressure, sleeping ten hours without water, and eating too many nuts nervously the first and second nights, and there you have it. The making of a visit—face-first—to good old Mother Earth.

Another desert rule: From 7:00 a.m. to 7:00 p.m., do not move!

EARLY AFTERNOON

I'm huddled up under my clothes and mosquito hat. There are so many flies buzzing and landing on me that I can't even read.

"That's it!" I said. And I started killing flies—about five or six. All of a sudden they were gone. I killed only what must have been half of the regulars, but it seemed to scare the rest off—or maybe they went for reinforcements?

At least I have five minutes of peace! I can even take off my hat, and it is so much cooler without that hat! I feel open and free again. No net between the desert and me. I must admit I feel a little guilty about killing the flies.

"If you leave me alone," I said out loud to no one except fly ears, "I'll leave you alone."

I can actually listen to the birds now that I'm not being buzzed constantly.

7:30 P.M.

I had my first sandstorm today. It wasn't a *Lawrence of Arabia* type of sandstorm because the sand here is not really fine; it's very rocky. Still, small pebbles pelted me while finding their way into everything from the pages of my books and backpacks to my ears and eyes. When I climbed out of my cave and up to the plateau during the sandstorm, I watched where I put my feet and hands, because bugs of all types were seeking refuge and clinging to small footholds along the cliff. There was a sense of kinship with them because I saw all life struggling to survive. Then something grabbed at my leg. I yelled and swatted at it, thinking it was a snake. Looking down, I saw it was just a wasp that had hopped onto my leg after I mistakenly stepped into his hiding spot. He wasn't trying to hurt me; he just needed something to cling to. He looked as surprised to see me as I was to see him.

day 5

I opened my eyes to see the stars were gone. It was morning already. "But it can't be," I told myself, "because I'm still tired." I rolled over on my right shoulder. "Ow!" I called out as the pain seared through my shoulder. When I passed out the other day, I also scraped up my shoulder pretty badly. My shirt keeps rubbing against it (which hurts), and I can't lie on my right side.

I looked up at the sky again, angry that the stars were gone. I have to get up. But I want to sleep. Sleep? If I sleep, I will pay the penalty. In an hour the sun will come crashing into my tent, and I will awake hot and sweating. Then I will sweat even more profusely as I hurry to get my gear together in order to get out of this saunalike tent. Then I'll step out of my tent into what—110-degree heat? And so what does sleeping later get me? It only leads to more suffering, and any hurrying I do after I get up only increases the discomfort, and what are the benefits? I get to go into the shade of my cave, which must be ninety or a hundred degrees, a minute or two earlier? But that minute or two of rushing costs me *anxiety* and *body hurry*, which equals greater heat. There must be a formula for that:

$$(body\ hurry + anxiety) \times minutes = more\ time$$
$$of\ miserable\ sweating$$

$$(relaxed\ body\ and\ mind) \times minutes = less\ time\ of\ miserable$$
$$sweating$$

So I got up right away, even though I'd slept like hell. My bed felt different last night even though I made it the same way: two thin yoga mats with a sleeping bag over them and then a sheet. But last night I felt every stone under my tent. And the ground! The ground was radiating heat until well after midnight. It was like a furnace in there. But what were my choices? I couldn't go to my cave after dark, because without a mosquito net, I'd be dead meat in my cave. Suddenly I find myself getting annoyed at Tamir—*where's my mosquito net!* But I realize it isn't his fault; it's mine. We bought a large mosquito net on the day he tried to show me different sites, and I forgot it at a grocery store.

But I want to be angry! And at someone or something. The flies—that's it, be mad at the flies. But there are none around right now. Where's a good fly when you need one? I try getting angry at Tamir again, but it's not his fault. Finally, I feel like a child throwing a tantrum. I get out of my tent and start to make coffee. A few mosquitoes start buzzing me as I pour water. I'm hurrying again.

"If I can just get this done," I tell myself, "and get away from them, it will be all right."

But that's a lie. It's not going to get better, because I'm the problem. And back in my tent when I realize I can't get away from my surroundings or my irritations, I watch myself throw a tin cup here and a water bottle there. I go out to the coffee again and quickly zip up the tent. I'm paranoid about bugs getting in, because even if it's open for only a few seconds, a couple of ants and flies and mosquitoes will find their way in.

Where's the friggin' water pitcher? I say to myself as I look around for it. I'm so frustrated that I can feel my eyes start to bug out of my head. Just as I'm ready to scream, I accidentally kick it over. It was right at my feet the whole time. I'm really ready to explode; to quit; to destroy the whole thing . . .

But the realization that I was starting to go crazy over a water pitcher and that it was at my feet the whole time elicits a chuckle, and its point is so well taken that it punctures my swelled-up sense of frustrated self. Deflated, I continue to laugh, then take a deep breath and go back to my morning chores.

But since I am constantly interrupted by renewed flashes of anger and frustration, I am forced to meditate almost constantly. First, I focus on filling the water bottles. Then I notice I hate doing this. I see that I am angry and notice my body is tense and my breathing uneven. I see these things and breathe—then I go back to the water bottles. I attend to the sound of the water poured into the bottle; I feel the sensation of holding it in my hand. I'm aware that I'm standing there. I feel tension creep back into my body, and I get frustrated at having to do this! Then I start my awareness practice all over again. It goes on like this all morning.

Last night I went for a couple of short walks. They were short because the flies kept attacking.

You know what I hate?

I hate the sound a mosquito makes as it zeros in on you, as

it looks for a place to sting. It's a high-pitched sound, and it makes me anxious. Why do they do that?

It reminds me of the Nazi Luftwaffe during World War II. They intentionally put a sound in their planes so that when they were dive-bombing you, you heard them coming. It increased the terror of their victims.

Even when I urinate, I find myself hurrying up in order to get out of the hot sun.

Hurrying only makes it worse. It increases the tension in my body. Actually, it isn't the hurry; it's the worry that's often hidden inside the hurry. I'll watch that; if I have to hurry, I'll see if I can let go of the worry.

I just realized a wonderful thing! Here in the desert, there are not just one or two kinds of bugs that bite. No! There are more than that. How wonderful to realize that profound and comforting thought. Let's see, the little red ants bite me, mosquitoes bite me, and then there's an even smaller mosquitolike bug that bites me. But wait! Oh, great joy! Look at the positive side. The flies, all ten gazillion of them, do not bite. They only drive me crazy with their constant company and chatter. Actually, this sounds a bit like relationships. You marry either someone who bites or someone who chatters too much.

I'm swearing—using curse words much more than usual. I wonder if Jesus ever swore during his forty days. Did he always talk politely to the devil? Did he love the flies and mosquitoes? Do you think he swatted them occasionally?

I once read about a monk who was so holy that the flies left him alone. That story makes me feel inadequate.

It's been so hot that I've wanted to strip down, but the flies won't allow it. I suppose Jesus was naked at times in the desert—maybe often. Since he had grown up dealing with flies, I'm sure he barely noticed they were there, even as they crawled about his face and body.

Sixteen years ago, when I lived in Nepal for a year, I saw many Nepalese people who didn't seem bothered when flies crawled and buzzed about their faces. The babies sat quietly while flies crawled all over them, and no one did anything. Flies were an accepted consequence of being alive, sort of like thoughts, emotions, and body sensations; from earliest memory we remember them as part of us, but they are not our essential being. Instead, thoughts, emotions, and body sensations are happenings within our being.

In Nepal, there is a blindness caused by a disease called trachoma, which is transmitted by flies. By accepting the flies and not swatting them away, the Nepalese have unwittingly subjected themselves to unnecessary blindness. If my thoughts, emotions, and body sensations are like flies, have they also brought with them a certain kind of blindness?

EARLY AFTERNOON

I am learning to read the desert. For example, the flies are heat forecasters. Today was the hottest day yet, and the flies were active earlier than usual. I've learned that the earlier in the day they attack, the hotter the day will be.

My original plan was to remain at my desert site for the forty days, but when Tamir couldn't come because of a punctured eardrum, I decided to hike to the hostel and get a mosquito net from Ya'el. She wasn't home, but she had said I could take the one off her door. Once there, I filled up my water bottles and then hiked back to my cave. I told myself that Jesus must have left his solitude at times—at least to find water.

LATE AFTERNOON

During a sandstorm something was blown into my ear. I could feel it crawling. It was crawling deeper into my ear—not out. I freaked, grabbed a water bottle, and squirted water into my ear six or seven times. I didn't see anything come out, but I hope whatever was in there did.

Then I went to the cliff above my cave, sat on a rock, and watched the wind blow clean the sky over the Dead Sea. Several years before, I had been to the Dead Sea, and it was a big letdown. I had anticipated being blown away by the Dead Sea because it had the aura of the Middle East, of the Old Testament, and of Jesus. Sodom and Gomorrah are believed to lie beneath the Dead Sea. When I first saw it, I was struck by how huge it is, 50 miles long, 395 square miles, and very blue. I got off our tour bus and ran to the sea. I jumped in and—

yuck!—a mouthful of salt. It was so salty that it burned my
eyes and lips; much saltier than any ocean—seven times as
salty as the ocean. And if a sea fish is put into the Dead Sea, it
dies fast. It wasn't really salt water either; it was more of a
watered salt. No wonder you float; it was as if you were actually just lying on a pile of salt. Anyway, after I made this all-
day pilgrimage to the Dead Sea and jumped in, burning my
eyes and lips, I floated for a minute or two and said, "That's
interesting." Then I got out and lounged at the Dead Sea cafe-
teria eating hamburgers and fries for an hour or so until my
bus was ready to leave.

As I sat on the rock and contemplated the irony of how
something so alive and blue can actually be so dead, I frequently
looked down at my feet, because a scorpion might have been
under the rock I was sitting on. The scorpions freak me out so
much that often I just stand up even when I'm tired. That's why
I want a lawn chair! Nothing extravagant, just something I can
see through so that I can see the scorpions coming and they
can't sneak up on me. Scorpions are mentioned in Luke 10:19:
"Behold, I give you the authority to trample on serpents and
scorpions . . ." (NKJV). But I don't feel like I've been given that
authority yet.

Anyway, while I sat on the cliff and looked down, checking
for scorpions, I saw a key next to my left foot. I bent down and
picked it up. It looked like a key for a file cabinet or a safe. I
couldn't help but think there was some kind of meaning in my
finding it. Maybe in this desert I will find the key to my life.

A few years ago, I went snorkeling off the coast of Hawaii. I
swam out about three hundred yards from shore, and during my
return, in about fifteen feet of water, I saw a key at the bottom

of the ocean. I dived once, then twice, without success. On the third dive, I managed to grab the key, and, looking at it, I was amazed to find it was the key to my car. I had dropped it swimming away from shore but found it on my return.

9:30 P.M.

I got the fly thing licked with that mosquito net, but now the red ants come in—and bite me. They bit me four times today.

As I lie in bed listening to the sounds of the desert—many of which I can't identify—I think about that show *The X-Files*. Don't weird things often happen in the desert on that show? I'm trying not to think about that too much.

I saw the lights of a plane hovering in the sky. It moved away, and then I heard two explosions. I hope they're not bombing anyone.

day 6

Today I'm in the cave by 6:30 a.m. Eventually I plan to be meditating and praying in it by 4:00 a.m. I'm slowly building up the time I officially meditate and pray. I say *officially* because I'm praying and meditating at set times each day, and yet throughout the day I continue praying in various ways. For example, one of the *un*official ways I meditate during the day is that when I'm hot and sweaty, and start getting angry, I'll suddenly catch myself and see what I'm doing. That means I've seen what I've started and what I'm promoting. Then I'll stop myself from going down that road, and then I'll even let go of the idea of stopping. Then a gap or opening occurs. It's a gap in time, a space between thoughts that continues opening itself right into the ego and beyond until you're in the place where communion with God is seen and experienced. That's one way of experiencing what Jesus experienced when he said, "I and the Father are one" (John 10:30 NASB); "You are in me, and I am in you" (John 14:20); and "The kingdom of God is within you" (Luke 17:21).

We, too, can have Jesus's experience of God, because he said, "I have set you an example" (John 13:15), and Jesus was smart enough not to set examples for us that were impossible. Jesus also said, "The person who trusts me will not only do what I'm doing but even greater things" (John 14:12 MSG).

Jesus doesn't lie.

I cried a lot in my morning meditation. About what? Mostly it doesn't matter. When I cry, pictures appear before me of sad things: people dying, my own pain, the world's pain—but most of the time in prayer and meditation, things come to my mind in order to be released, to pass away and bring change.

The Gospel of Mark tells us that Mary Magdalene cared for the needs of Jesus, and yet after Jesus's resurrection he told her, "Do not cling to Me" (John 20:17 NKJV). So in my meditations, I care for my needs and my grief by giving them my attention, and yet I try not to cling.

Throughout the day, short moments of Spirit are beginning to arise. They seem to come when I don't cling to Jesus or reflections of God or eternity or the limitless. Paul wrote that "the Spirit Himself bears witness with our spirit" (Romans 8:16 NKJV). The Spirit of God within me doesn't cling; it's the scared human being that does, and this fearful clinging gets between God and me. It splits the Spirit in half until it can't recognize itself. But when I don't cling, Spirit naturally arises and bears witness to and knows itself.

While I meditate, I hear many sounds of nature—birds, lizards, and various bugs. Sometimes they're new, interesting, or pleasant sounding. At other times, they're a repetitive disturbance—noisy. In my meditation I watch my thoughts. They are just like the sounds of nature. Sometimes interesting and pretty; at other times disturbing, noisy, and repetitive.

Tamir had talked about "blending in," about sitting on a rock and "becoming the rock." As I walk along the boulders and sand, thoughts of myself leave me until I am face-to-face with the desert. But since thoughts of myself have left me, *there is only one face.*

My forehead is scabbing over pretty well, but on my shoulder the wound is a bit yellow. I hope it's not infected. Maybe Tamir can tell me when he visits tomorrow.

Also, I'm really missing women, especially since there is nothing better than having a loving woman dress and soothe your wounds. If my friend Bonnie, who is an ex-girlfriend, were here, I know she would take care of me. But then again, that's one of the reasons our romantic relationship ended. I was looking for a woman to love and take care of me, and yet I didn't want her to take care of me too much. That kind of confusion is death to a relationship, and I guess that is part of the reason I'm here: to dress and soothe my own wounds—the spiritual and emotional, and now even the physical. I've found if I do it myself—at least somewhat—then my relationships with others (especially women) become less obsessive, less addictive, less of a "using of them," and changes into a preference, a way to connect, share vulnerability, and be genuinely fond of each other. I can actually love others more fully when I'm not addictively using them to fill my own inner lack of love. Don't get me wrong; we all need to lean on one another sometimes and to be loved when we feel unloved—but not all the time.

I'm developing a "bug system." I can keep most of the bugs out now that I have a small two-and-a-half-by-five-foot mosquito net, but when some ants and flies sneak in, I capture them in a Ziploc baggie and keep them in it until next time I open the mosquito net.

I prefer catching them to killing them because I don't feel good killing them. It's good not to wantonly kill things, because it makes me so much more conscious of killing things when I occasionally have to. The problem with killing small things unconsciously is that we tend to move up the food chain until we're killing each other in the same unconscious way we kill an ant. But if we cherish all life from the get-go, then killing is hard to do because it hurts our hearts—and killing should be hard to do. If killing is ever easy, then it must be because we've already killed a part of our own hearts. At the same time, Joseph Campbell said, "All life lives on other life," and even Jesus enjoyed a good broiled fish now and then.

8:30 P.M.

I killed a bunch of flies again. It started because I felt like a prisoner inside this mosquito net. For almost thirteen hours I stayed in this thirty-by-fifty-five-inch net prison. The net is high enough to sit in meditation posture and long enough to lie down, provided I keep my knees up and bent. But I'd had enough. I was tired of seeing the beautiful landscape of the Judean desert through a net. So I opened the net and looked at my surroundings.

"Ah, yes," I said, overcome by my surroundings. "How beautiful."

Then the flies attacked. They wouldn't even allow me five minutes of peaceful appreciation of the desert. Five or six of them landed on me almost immediately, climbing up my nose, zeroing in on my wounds, and chewing on the scabs. I killed three of them, and then it was quiet—peaceful. Then fifteen minutes later they returned with reinforcements, and it went on like this for an hour. I'd kill one or two and they'd leave me alone, and then I could appreciate the Judean hills, the blue sky, and the Dead Sea until they'd return. Eventually I got tired of the carnage and went back into my mosquito net. They buzzed loudly as they landed on the outside of my net, angrily waiting for me to come out.

I went to *the edge* alone for the first time today, which is the edge of a 250-foot cliff just below my cave. During the winter rains, the water flows down three wadis up on the plateau and converges just above my cave. For millions of years, it has rushed down and through the limestone until it carved out my cave. Then the rushing water continues on, descending for another hundred feet or so before it reaches the edge of the cliff. That's the edge I went to, and that's where the waterfall starts.

I first went to the edge with Tamir the Wednesday before I started my forty days. It was a spectacular site, with rock faces to my left and right, the cliff dropping off before me, and the

Dead Sea about a mile in the distance. It was also disorienting and scary. Tamir picked a spot right at the edge and sat on it as comfortably and confidently as I do when I sit next to a swimming pool. When I saw him do that, combined with how afraid I was—well, I was hooked, drawn to *the edge* by what I did and didn't understand.

Tamir's girlfriend, Ya'el, had sat at the edge of a two-thousand-foot cliff on the day she took me to other sites after Tamir punctured his eardrum. She sat there nonchalantly, sunning herself like some southern belle drinking mint juleps with one hand while fanning herself with the other.

"Oh? Why, that little ole canyon would never hurt a fly," she'd say.

I stayed well back from her that day as I peered over into the abyss (well, okay, it wasn't really an abyss; I could see the bottom)—but still, I felt dizzy, disoriented, like I could lose my balance and equilibrium at any time and fall sideways into the canyon. It felt a bit like when I was a child, spinning and whirling myself into a disorientation. I teetered this way and that until I fell over like a drunken sailor, only to get up and do it again and again. But of course every child learns that disorientation is not without risk when the inevitable happens and they fall into a coffee table—cracking their head—and crying until Mama picks them up.

But there was no mama here, and that two-thousand-foot cliff was not a coffee table.

"It scares me for some reason," I said to Ya'el.

Now, admitting my fear was no small feat in itself. It was a direct result of years of therapy and many dollars. Without that therapy, I would have choked off any fear and gone to the edge rigid as a board while not feeling anything. "Big deal," I would have said, looking over the edge and never letting on to myself or anyone else that I was afraid.

(It just dawned on me how crazy I am, how crazy people are. I had to go to therapy and spend thousands of dollars in order to say, "I'm afraid.")

Anyway, Ya'el did reply to my admission of fear, but I don't remember what she said. Even if I did remember, it wouldn't have mattered, because she was still sitting on the edge of a two-thousand-foot cliff. And nothing she could have said would have conveyed to me that it was okay to be sitting on the edge of that two-thousand-foot cliff.

But Ya'el's a tough cookie. Just two years ago she was a wife in an ultraconservative Jewish group here in Israel. She had to wear a scarf or hat and cover her hair every time she left the house. She could only speak with people in her religious sect.

So in many ways she had already been to the edge—pushed to the edge of what she could tolerate, the edge of her beliefs, the edge of her social group and her religion. She was pushed to the edge and saw that she had to make a choice. Life or death? To stay within the life she had known was death to her. So one day Ya'el went to the edge of her life and looked back at how she was living. "Enough!" she said. Then she jumped over the edge, dead to the old life and born into the new.

Now she is part of the Jewish renewal movement in Israel. She has all kinds of spiritual books in her room, dolphin statues on her shelves, and dolphin pictures on her walls. Her room smells of incense, and she's become a healer, using flower remedies and herbs. She also said I was "an alien."

"An alien?" I asked.

"Yes," she said. "You have a different energy—like an alien."

Even if Ya'el was right and I was an alien, I still wanted to know why I had such a fear of the edge. And why did I have such strange notions of actually jumping off? And why, when I saw her near the edge, did I have the weird thought of pushing her over the edge?

We all have an edge. A place we won't go near or look beyond. Or don't want to look into. Or admit is there. That's why I'm here in the desert for forty days, to meet my edge and go past it. The even deeper reason is to confront God. To meet my God-edge and go beyond. Did you ever notice how many people never confront or go to their God-edge? They never go to the edge of who they think God is and then past that edge into a new place and a new edge and a new way of seeing God. God has no permanent edge; the only edges to God are the ones human beings put there. And that's why Jesus said, "The Son of Man has no place to lay his head" (Matthew 8:20).

There was no place where God's edge began or ended for Jesus, no edge on which Jesus could lay his head. And that's why if you ever know Jesus deeply enough, you won't see him sitting at an edge or in one place only. Instead, you will see him continually moving within the edgeless Being of God, walking more deeply into God's presence while beckoning us to follow.

I decided to stay in my mosquito net till 8:30 p.m. because my tent is a sauna until about 2:00 a.m. But at 8:00 p.m. I heard something. It was a hum that started low and got louder. *Is that a siren? Here in the desert? Some kind of plane or a flock of birds flying overhead?* I looked up, but I didn't see birds. It was then that I realized it was the sound of mosquitoes starting their engines in the large crack of my cave. The lizard, who shares my cave and whom I call Sandy (because he's sand colored), started "clucking" loudly. He knew something was up. I threw everything into my duffel bag as quickly as possible while remembering not to bump my head on the rock ceiling. Then I made a mindful dash out of my net.

I climbed out from the cave and up to the plateau, while throwing the duffel bag up and out ahead of me. At the last minute, I saw Sandy, my lizard friend, or one of his relatives, but it was too late. I scared the heck out of him. My duffel bag just missed squashing him. I walked quickly to my tent. Once inside I looked at my thermometer and saw that it was a hundred degrees. It's 8:30 p.m., and it's a hundred degrees in my tent! This is it! I've had enough! I'm going to ask Tamir to help me. Even if he is Mr. Bare-Bones Desert Guy, I'm going to tell him I need a few things. This forty days in the desert is hard enough and will get harder.

I need a cot! So I can lie down and keep cool. The ground is just too hot. It retains the heat long after the air has cooled.

I need a chair! The "scorpion under every rock I sit on" anxiety just isn't cutting it. With a chair, I can sit outside at night when it's really windy (wind blows away the mosquitoes) and look up at the stars.

And finally, *I need the biggest freakin' mosquito net they make.* If I'm going to be under that net for thirteen to fourteen hours, at least let me straighten out my legs.

To make matters worse, the flies started biting me today, whereas before they just buzzed me.

Bite count today:

2 fly bites
+ 4 ant bites
+ 3 mosquito stings
= 9 total bites or stings today

I saw my first snake today after I went to *the edge* for the first time alone. As I climbed back up the cliffs toward my cave, I saw what looked like a yellow bungee cord. I figured the winter floods must have washed it here. But when I got closer, it slithered away. It was yellow with black stripes.

"Black and yellow," Tamir said, "are Mother Nature's way of saying 'dangerous fellow.'"

I respected the bungee cord's wishes to have some space, and I went the other way. I also found two chewed-off legs in a cave. All that's left of an ibex? And what about the animal that ate him? Will he eat me?

While I lay in bed reading with the light on, I heard intermittent raindrops on my tent—a couple every few seconds. I sat up and shined my flashlight through the fabric of my tent. The tent was covered with hundreds of bugs. *It's raining bugs!* For a moment I'm worried. *Will they chew through the fabric like*

swarms of grasshoppers or locusts, leaving me naked and unprotected beneath the stars? But as they continued to land, my concern turned into annoyance. I shut off the light, lay back down, and closed my eyes. *I've had enough bugs for one day. I'm going to bed.*

day 7

I woke up in an angry mood. I dreamed about "Frasier," the sitcom psychiatrist. He was at a Volvo dealer, and he was throwing a fit!

"I make buckets of money!" he said. "And I can't afford one of these Volvos!"

Oddly enough, they weren't Volvo cars; they were Volvo desks and tables. There was nothing special about them, and they were cheaply made. In the dream I grabbed one to see if it felt like particleboard—it did.

I didn't drink any coffee today. So if I'm boring, that's why. I'm going to go three days without coffee, but if Tamir comes, I may have some, because I'm kind of blah when I'm going through withdrawal. Maybe I'll stay off coffee if I find I'm just as creative, meaning if my journal entries are not boring.

My world is moving in on me. If you've done silent retreats or spent time alone, you know what I mean. Many of the distractions I've used to control my world and myself are not available here in the desert. For example, there's no television, no radio, nothing to read except the few Bibles I brought and my book. I don't mean any offense, but the Bible got boring after an hour or so, especially the Old Testament.

Exercise and exploration of the landscape can be another distraction, but the heat weakens me so much that it prevents me from being active. Instead, I just want to lie in my cave, motionless like a rock. Any movement at all, and I feel heat being generated. If I get too frustrated, heat's generated. I can actually watch how my different thoughts create a hotter response in my body.

Meanwhile, I am so listless and bored that I often talk to Sandy the lizard.

"Do you ever catch a fly, Sandy?" I ask. "I've only seen you eat bugs that are so small that I can't even see them.

"I bet a fly would be a whole day's food for you. I bet it rarely happens, like a hole-in-one in golf. Do you remember the catching of a fly in the same way a golfer remembers a hole-in-one?

"'Yep,' you'll say someday to your buddies in the salamander retirement home, 'I remember back in '83 when I got myself a fly . . .'

"Do you have to buy them all drinks after getting a fly?"

Sandy stops about a foot away, right above me. He clings to the rock wall and looks directly at me.

"Sandy," I say, and his ears, those little lumps on the sides of his head, indent for a moment.

"Sandy," I say again, and sure enough, his head indents again. I call his name three more times, and each time his head nearly collapses. But then I call his name again, and he doesn't react. I say it again; still no reaction. I try again; no response. Oh no! Sandy, my only friend in this cave, has stopped listening to me.

I just got bit by some kind of midget bug with wings I haven't seen before.

The flies are ticked off. I don't kill them anymore, but their inability to get at me in my mosquito net seems to frustrate them. I swear I can hear anger in their buzzing, and without this mosquito net, I'd be a dead man. The flies have patterns, and they're organized. They usually harass me for fifteen minutes at a time, then depart, only to return after another fifteen or twenty minutes. This pattern repeats itself throughout the day.

They usually attack me in pairs. When I killed a fly the other day, his companion landed next to him, nudged him, and tried to help him fly away. I felt bad after seeing that. Right now there are three or four pairs of them buzzing around and landing on my net. I also found that when I am quiet and at ease, the flies are less worked up and less likely to harass me—*but they still do.*

I'm especially exhausted today. It was hot! Tamir never showed up with my larger mosquito net or gas for my stove. I had looked forward to eating noodles tonight. Instead, I ate a couple of Clif Bars and fell asleep.

day 8

I am one-fifth of the way through. In two more days, I will be one-fourth of the way done! The winds started at 4:10 p.m. today. The ants came out at 4:15 p.m. I still cannot believe how remarkably well I'm taking how miserable it is here. It would be a hundred times better if there weren't any flies. It would be really cool then—hot—but cool! I wonder what the flies want from me? Do they seek the salt or minerals in my sweat? Do they eat something off my skin?

I called Tamir last night and told him I need a cot. I am so weak and exhausted all the time that it is hard to pray or meditate. I sit anywhere from twenty to forty-five minutes when I meditate in the cave. I can't sit longer because the boulders on which I sit hurt my legs. My knees also hurt from being half bent and scrunched up in the mosquito net all the time. I've noticed that there are downtimes for the flies, and that's when I stretch my legs. I can leave the net open for up to fifteen minutes before the flies start attacking me. I especially hate looking out through the net, because all of life has a grid over it. The beautiful blue sky, the rocky brown cliffs, my buddy Sandy—all have a fuzzy grid over them. Whenever I step out of or open the mosquito net—all appears clear. The ego is like that; it's a net that is instantly thrown over whatever we turn our attention to. It controls and distorts everything.

Anyway, when I phoned Tamir last night, he asked, "What was so urgent about you needing a cot?" He almost sounded disappointed in me, like I had I let him down because I didn't want to endure nature and blend with her his way. I don't think he understands. I'm not an expert camper who likes to rough it. And roughing it isn't my priority. Spending forty days in the desert is my first priority. The next priority is spending it in the Judean desert. Third is isolation. After that, I don't care too much. But so far, it has really turned out to be a harsh test in a difficult environment.

I went to *the edge* again. Actually, I kind of crawled to the edge, because it looks too easy to trip near it. And if I were to trip, then "bye-bye" over the edge I'd go. As I climbed back up to my cave, a very fat mouse ran by.

"Hey, Mister Mouse," I called after him. "You won't be around long if you don't know how to hide better than that!"

I guess I'm turning into a kind of desert Dr. Dolittle. I'm talking to all the animals. When I saw a large black beetle walking along, I told him I had seen his cousin the other day.

"He was stuck in a hole and trying to get out," I told him. "I hope he's okay."

3:30 A.M.

Bark!

I woke up with a start. I had distinctly heard a bark. Was it a hyena? A wolf? I barked back to let it know I was here.

"You'd better not come near here," my bark said.

When I told Tamir the next day, I was sheepishly disappointed when he said it was probably "only a little fox."

When I told Tamir how I was learning not to hurry or make quick movements because I only got hotter, he said, "The bedouins say, 'To hurry is the devil.'"

Then he asked about the rocks I piled by the wadi in order to mark my campsite.

"Because that's a bedouin thing," he said. "That's how bedouins mark their territory."

"Yeah," I said, feeling the intense pleasure of knowing that I, Bill Elliott, was kind of a bedouin.

Tamir looked at me curiously. "Did Ya'el tell you to do that, or did you think of it yourself?"

I immediately deflated before his eyes and said, "Ya'el said to do it."

"That's a big tent you have," Tamir said. "A whole family could stay in that!"

I didn't know if it was a subtle disapproval or criticism on his part, but I tended to shrink a little whenever he made comments like that.

"See that spot," he said, pointing to a clump of rocks.

"I would sleep there," he said. "I'd just throw my pad and sleeping bag down—and sleep there."

"I'm not much of a camper," I told Tamir.

"I know," he said. "It took me a few days to figure that out."

Then Tamir saw one of my plastic bottles lying on the ground near my tent. He bent down to pick it up.

"Don't pick up that bottle," I said. "That's my pee bottle. I use it in the middle of the night when I'm in my tent and I don't want to go outside."

Tamir looked at me—stunned. "You mean you don't want to go outside in the middle of the night to pee?"

He had been waiting for me at my cave when I returned from the edge. With his long jet-black beard, Tamir looked like a Grecian Formula Moses.

"I have ice water and grapes for you with a few apricots," he said. Then I remembered our conversation from a few days before when Tamir had asked, "Is it okay if I bring you an offering?"

I had felt funny then, because in India and Nepal they brought offerings to yogis and holy men who inhabit caves. Was I now one of them? A yogi? A holy man? I had a mental picture of people placing offerings at my feet while I gave them blessings in return—that is, if I felt like it.

"What?" I asked Tamir, just a bit freaked out by my own imaginings.

"Can I bring you some pears or something?" Tamir asked. "I just really appreciate what you're doing."

And now here he was handing me some fruit, and as he did I imagined love streaming out from my heart to him. Then I told him excitedly of my realizations and described the animals I had seen.

"There was a pair of giant white birds gliding across the sky with black-tipped wings," I said.

"That was an Egyptian vulture," he replied. "And that was a swallow nest in your cave—but those aren't swallow droppings in your cave. That's from a bigger bird—a pigeon perhaps.

"That little bird you saw by the edge of the cliff was a blackstart.

"That's not a salamander; that's a gecko in your cave.

"And this tree over here makes a fine coal—it burns very hot. This is the same bush that Hagar of the Bible put Ishmael under."

Then he bent over and touched a plant.

"See this flower—the bedouins use it to make candles," he said. Then he proceeded to peel off the green stem, and inside was a long white string.

"Since it grows out of a rock, it's called 'rock's wool.' And it's used as a wick. All you have to do is put it in some olive oil, and you have a candle."

"How do I get the wick to stand up in the olive oil?" I asked.

He paused. "I don't know," he replied.

Hey, I finally stumped him, I thought.

But then he said, "Why don't you try making a candle and find out for yourself!"

I also told him about the two lower goat legs I found in a cave down by the edge.

"Probably a wolf," he said. "But don't worry, because the

wolves in this desert are all lone wolves. There's not enough food around to support packs of wolves."

Besides the fruit and ice water, he dropped off an air mattress, olive oil, pita bread, a cot, and . . . drum roll, please . . . *some nondairy creamer*!

After he left, I started yelping and singing. I held up the can of nondairy creamer and sang, "I've got creamer! I've got creamer! I've got creamer!"

Then I grabbed a pita bread and opened the bottle of olive oil. Since I didn't have a plate to pour the olive oil on, I just bit into the pita I had in my right hand and then took a swig from the bottle of olive oil I had in my left hand. I walked over and stood on the plateau with my left foot up on a rock and watched the sun go down while tearing off pieces of pita with my teeth and washing them down with slugs of olive oil. I felt like a bold adventurer, a wild drunken sailor who was drinking olive oil straight from the bottle. I basked in the glory of the moment.

"Your cave is so big," Tamir had said, "it's like a villa."

I didn't like his making my cave sound luxurious. It wasn't, and I wanted to feel like I was roughing it a bit. But he did bring my cot! Why did I need a cot? Because you could fry an egg on the floor of my tent till almost midnight. A cot is off the ground. I'm sure Jesus would have used a cot if he had one. Jesus didn't mind living the good life, and unlike John the Baptist, who fasted and lived on locusts, Jesus was called a glutton and a drunkard by his critics. So I think a cot would have been okay with him.

I went outside at 10:00 p.m. The stars are so wondrous. How could anyone look up at them and think there is no intent behind it all? Anyway, it seems such a pity that I will die in four or five decades. When I look up at the stars, I want to visit every one of them!

day 9

This is a no-coffee day, so if I sound low on energy, that's why. Even so, I'm ecstatic because my new mosquito net is palatial compared to the old one. It's probably seven feet long, three and a half feet wide, and four feet high. I can now stretch out my legs and lie down. Earlier this morning, I began to talk with the shorts I had tossed down by my feet. Now that my legs were stretched out, my feet seemed so far away.

"Hey, Mr. Shorts," I called out. "Can you hear me all the way over there?"

The mosquito net is a wonderful invention. I bet when it first came out thousands of years ago, everybody just had to have one. I wonder if they ever considered covering a whole city with a mosquito net.

It didn't take long before I felt guilty. Maybe my mosquito net was too luxurious. Was I having it too easy now? Shouldn't I be suffering more? *When things get this good*, I thought, *they never come without a price.*

"Pitiful," a voice said.

"Who said that?" I asked.

"I said it," the voice said again. "And you're pitiful."

"Who said . . ."

"You're talking to yourself, you idiot," the voice said, "and you're pitiful because you just can't accept the good that's given to you without feeling guilty or afraid."

I'm afraid I'm wasting my time in the desert. Maybe I should be on my hands and knees, calling on God to appear on some cloud or in a dramatic way.

Then Jesus says, "Bill, just be with me."

Since I know Jesus's essence is everywhere, both inside and out, I relax until "I am."

I thought about past lovers a lot today. I am remembering the times we had and having imaginary conversations with them. My energy is really picking up, which happens in deep meditation or prayer. It is a physical experience that mirrors the spiritual ecstasy that comes from letting go into a passionate union with the Divine.

Life is short. I looked at the cliffs, my cave, all the stones, boulders, and rocks; they were here before me—way before me—and will be here long after I'm gone. I'm barely a speck in time, yet I think I'm so important.

Later, I imagine myself on my deathbed. I look up at God as I'm dying and say, "I don't really want to come back here—it was too hard.

"The only way you could sucker me into coming back," I say, "is if you show me people suffering in one picture and then happy in another—that my life would have something to do with people suffering less because I was here."

I mean, a big car, a sexy wife, and lots of money aren't bringing me back, because I've seen the trade-offs. But if I do come back in order to help others, then I'd be willing to take the big car, sexy wife, and lots of money too.

My cave is really more like a big overhang with a massive stone pillar forty to fifty feet in circumference. As I lie on my back and look up at how I managed to tie the mosquito net to the ceiling—well, there are many stories there. I used twine and nylon rope along with part of a mangled bicycle rack I found among the rocks down by the edge. It must have been washed here by the floods. I also used a two-foot-long rod I found and—most important of all—duct tape. My friend Dave used to tell me to take duct tape with me whenever I went outdoors.

"You can use this stuff for just about anything, Wonder Brother," he said. He liked to call me "Wonder Brother," a name he made up for me when I was twenty years old because I always said, "I wonder why . . . ?"

I suppose just about anything in this world can be used to aid in giving life or inhibiting life. For example, my mind can be turned toward loving thoughts or judgmental and destructive thoughts. Often thoughts are used like Dave's duct tape, as a temporary way of fixing something. I've seen people overlay their negative thoughts with positive thoughts. They tell themselves, "I'm a good person," or "I'm a loving person," or "May all people be happy." But underneath they still have years of piled-up negative thoughts, like the garbage that's accumulated down by the edge's dried-up waterfall. So once these people stop manufacturing their positive thoughts, their old hateful, negative thoughts come back. It's like that dude who has to push the stone up the hill every day. Every night it rolls down again. So what I've begun to find is that under my positive thoughts are piles of negative thoughts, but under the negative thoughts are love, ease, and well-being. They were placed there as the foundation of what we are. I believe this is what Jesus meant when he told about "a man building a house, who dug down deep and laid the foundation on rock. When a flood came, the torrent struck that house but could not shake it" (Luke 6:48). Beneath all the "I think's" and "I do's" is the bedrock, the foundation of "I Am." A place that good works cannot create and that bad works can never, ever destroy. "The kingdom of God is within" (Luke 17:21), as Jesus said; it is a place of "I Am" where all sins have been forgiven and have always been forgiven.

It's dark, and I'm lying in bed. For some reason I woke up, and I haven't the slightest idea what time it is—I just know that it's after midnight and before sunrise. I turn onto my side, reach down next to my bed, and grab my flashlight. Turning it on, I point it at the ceiling and illuminate the key that I found several days ago as it hangs in the darkness. I tied it there to remind me—but of what?

Jesus talked about "the key to knowledge" (Luke 11:52) and said, "I will give you the keys of the kingdom of heaven; whatever you bind on earth will be bound in heaven, and whatever you loose on earth will be loosed in heaven" (Matthew 16:19).

But what key is he talking about? What key is the key to the kingdom of heaven that looses and binds in heaven and on earth?

That's why I came to the desert—to find that key. I turned off the flashlight and lay in the darkness. That's when it hit me: the key to the kingdom of heaven is death.

day 10

One-quarter of the way done! This morning I sat for an hour in my tent, which is so much easier than meditating in the cave.

Looking back on it, I guess you could say the key to my life has always been death. I first died in the fall of 1981. I didn't plan on dying or losing my life then, and since I didn't know the meaning of Jesus's words "Whoever loses his life . . . will find it" (Matthew 10:39), I tried to keep my life as I wanted it to be; but that was part of the problem, and that's why it was the key. But this key may ultimately have been worthless to me if not for my relationship with God.

My mother taught me very early about God. Not so much "God as a Father," but God as a loving, nurturing companion. Talking to God has always been as real to me as talking to the man next door. (Actually, I never talked to the man next door; I was afraid of him.)

I guess I was like any kid—I believed there was a God, and it seemed there definitely was a God when good things happened, like when I hit a home run in Little League to win the game. But when I struck out and we lost the game, where was God then?

Then when I was nine years old, my grandmother came to live with us because she was sick with cancer. Outside of my mother, there was no one I loved more than my grandmother. Eventually she died at home one night while I was in the next room.

"She's dead," I heard the grown-ups say, and as they said that, something clutched at my chest, and I couldn't breathe. I was stunned and shocked—unable to grasp the meaning of what I had just heard. They saw me struggling to breathe and came over to help. Eventually I was able to take a breath, but from that moment on I was different—and unable to say how or why. It was similar to when I was first taught to add and sub-tract, or to read. I looked at the numbers or letters and words in front of me, and my mind (this strange bio-magical process) started looking from all angles, trying to find the first under-standing upon which to build the rest of my understanding.

But I couldn't find the first understanding when my grand-mother died. And worse yet, when I looked to the adults around me to see if I could see the first understanding in their faces and eyes, I saw nothing. In fact, they all went about their business in a very strange way. Almost as if nothing at all had happened. But for me, something did happen. Something very big indeed. And I wanted to say to them, "Did you . . . did you see that?"

But I wasn't sure how to ask, and I wasn't sure what it was I was even asking about.

After my grandmother died, I went back to baseball, Little League, and watching the Cubs on television. Then a few years later my father got sick. He stayed home from work all the time and always wore pajamas. He'd had a major heart attack.

Then my mother got sick. She started lying on the couch a lot. She always seemed to be wearing her pajamas too. She had cancer.

The house I lived in changed from a vibrant, bright, and energetic house—where light breezes entered easily through open windows—to a house in which life seemed to be lived in slow motion; an inert, dark place where shadows and shadowy figures moved about. And the windows? They were always closed.

I knew something was happening, and I must have suspected something even bigger was going to happen. But this ominous premonition wasn't as clear to me then as I make it seem now. Instead, it was more like the tummy aches children get when they don't like school or aren't getting along with their class-mates; they're afraid, but they don't know how to express that, so they just have a tummy ache.

I had a tummy ache, and I suspect that in some unconscious way I knew my parents were sick in the same way my grandmother had been. And I saw what had happened to my grandmother—she died.

My father was the first to go. We had just finished talking when he stood up and started to gurgle.

"Are you okay?" I asked as he walked back to his room.

"Why, what's wrong?" he said, trying to act nonchalant about the fact that he was gasping for breath and his eyes were bugging out. Since then I have often wondered, was the denial of his condition an attempt to avoid thinking he was going to die? Or was it the last act of a caring father who sought to spare his son any worry or concern? After he died, once again I wanted to say to the adults around me, "Hey, did you see that? Did you see it this time?" But once again, it was business as usual for them.

My father had been the "hard one" in my family, while my mother was the "soft one." With the strength and security of the hard one gone, all I had was my mother—the soft one to cling to—and she was ill and getting sicker by the day. My mother died at home six months after my father. She was fifty-six years old, and I was twelve. She died with my praying hands on her head—trying to bring her back to life. I didn't have to ask anyone if they had seen that. The appropriate question would have been, "Do you see me?" Because I wasn't even sure I existed anymore.

"Can you please tell me if I exist?" I would have asked. "Because I think I may need to cry and be afraid—but I can't do those things if I don't exist."

"So tell me, please . . ."

That's why I came to the desert. Because when they died, I began to exist in a way that had no words, no sound, and no movement. And no one, I mean no one, could tell me with any authority where I was or what was happening.

Toward the end of my morning sitting, I cried a lot. I felt how much I really missed my friend Dave and all the other people who have died, especially my mother and grandmother—even my father. I guess when you're twelve years old and your parents die, you can't really acknowledge to what extent they're missed.

That would be too much to bear at that age. That need for nurturance and closeness, when not met, is heart- and soul-wrenching. To go on day after day, no longer being touched in the way that a mother touches, is a starvation of the body. The soul of a child would rather shut down than continually have those hungry heart longings unmet. So when I wept this morning, it was for that simple, ordinary thing: the touch and intimacy of a mother and the palpable connection to a friend. Of course, I am aware of their spiritual presence, but that doesn't fill every human need. There is nothing like the touch of a mother or the sharing and exchanges of one's life with an old friend who knows you. I can still feel the "wholeness" in my body when I remember my mother scratching my back or rubbing my head. The wholeness of knowing I always had a place to go and be safe.

I think of my friend Dave, the oldest friendship I had—more than twenty years. How he had actually been like a spiritual mentor to me. He first met me when he dated my sister twenty-three years ago.

"When I first saw you, Wonder Brother," Dave said, "you were rocking in your rocking chair and eating whole chickens."

He was right. When he first met me, I was really into lifting weights and eating whole chickens for the protein. I'd eat them, just as he said, as I rocked in my rocking chair. I was also driving a red sports car with the belief that if I was "cool" enough, somehow I would be happy. Dave questioned that belief, while carrying a guitar—complete with a Woodstock sticker—and a mandolin in the back of a '72 Ford Pinto that would have exploded if rear-ended.

"Wonder Brother," Dave liked to recall, "remember when you asked me, 'Dave, when you're stopped at a stoplight, and you're in your Ford Pinto next to a really nice car, do you think the guy looks over and thinks, *That guy is a geek?*"

When somebody like Dave kills himself, you go over it many times in your mind and ask, "What should I have done differently?" What if I would have fought through his attempts to push me away and . . . and then what? Taken control of his life for him? That would have been impossible, because my relationship with Dave was based on giving the other space and freedom and respecting how he chose to live his life.

The last few years before Dave got sicker, I didn't see him much. His narcissism had gotten worse, and he started saying nasty things to me and referring to me as "Mr. Elliott, who's famous for interviewing famous people." I thought he was just being a jerk. I didn't realize it was the beginning of a mental illness.

Previously, he had been an invaluable friend and critic of my writing. When Dave said something was good, I knew it was good. And when what I showed him wasn't good, he let me know in a nice way. But as he got sicker, he would just read something I wrote and say, "This sucks," and "This sucks," and "This sucks," as he turned page after page.

The few times I confronted him about his attitude, he'd apologize—but then do it again. Eventually we drifted apart, and the last time I saw him, he had picked up part of my manuscript on Jesus and waved it in front of my face, saying, "What is all this Jesus stuff about anyway, Mr. Elliott?"

But Dave was a lot like Jesus. They both loved the wilderness, and that's where they both went to get more deeply connected with God. Dave was also a schoolteacher, and like Jesus, he was very kind to children. He taught gym class and was outspoken about the other gym teachers who made the fat and uncoordinated kids do athletic things that humiliated them in front of other students. At Dave's funeral, I met a woman and her young daughter.

"Anna wanted to come because Dave was Anna's favorite teacher," the mother said.

Looking at Anna, who was a bit overweight, I could see she was just the type of kid Dave would have rescued from hellish gym classes and sadistic gym teachers. Yet it was his being a teacher that ultimately contributed to his death. Just like Jesus.

So, like Jesus, who was in the desert for forty days, and Moses, who was on the mountain with God for forty days, I'm spending forty days in solitude with the Spirit. Am I just supposed to wait? Should I do spiritual exercises that open, focus, ready, and attune me? Should I be praying more? Sitting in meditation more? Bowing more? Saying my "Jesus, have mercy" prayer/mantra more? Or should I just wait?

What did Jesus do? Did he pray for God to come? Did he do certain prayers or bow? Or did he just wait, knowing that God is always present and accepting whatever form that would take?

Is my constant but erratic effort at being present good enough?

Today I got a great idea. I'm going to excavate. I'm going to fill the spaces between these boulders on the floor of the cave with sand and flatten it out so I can sit and lie more comfortably. But won't the high winds just blow the sand away each night?

Nope! I've got another plan.

After I cried in meditation this morning, I felt angry. It was anger at God. I never asked to be born, despite what some of those New Age "create your own reality" types say. Besides, there must have been a time when you weren't created yet—so how could you have asked to be created? Anyway, you and I are born here without any say in the matter. Then we get close to people, and what happens next? Either we leave them or they leave us. Either we watch them die or they watch us die. Who thought up this mess?

My gecko friend, Sandy, is clucking away. Sometimes he picks up his tail and sticks out his butt as if he's going to fart—but I never hear anything. Sometimes he just turns his head and starts licking his rear.

I didn't put any bandages on my wounds for the first time since I passed out on the third day. I put my hand on the wound every day and align with Jesus's presence and then say, "Jesus, have mercy," three times. My forehead is healing in a way I would call "miraculous." My back and shoulder are still a bit scabby. The flies like to land there for a quick snack. I tried shooing one fly away from a scab, and he was just frozen there, so focused on his meal that he was willing to risk his life.

When Dave died a year ago, I took some of his gear and some of his clothes. For a month after he died, I wore some of his clothes, but I was finding myself so depressed that I stopped wearing them. Part of me thought in some strange way that his clothes might have some of "the energy of his depression and illness" on them, and it was affecting me. So I gave some away and kept the rest of his belongings back in my shed. Slowly, after some of grief's black, tarry emotion lifted, I began to wear a few things. Most of his clothes were geared for one of two things: camping and hiking, or running. At one time he was a triathlete, but eventually he only competed in running events. I took his hiking and camping gear while giving his running shoes to a homeless guy I knew. So if you see a homeless guy with an eighty-dollar pair of Nikes, you know where he got them. I kept Dave's new hiking boots. But what about his almost-new sleeping bag? Should I sleep in his sleeping bag? What if I found myself sleeping in the same mental illness he had?

When Ya'el and then Tamir took me to the edge of the cliff, I saw how easy it would be to end it, to end any present and future misery in my life. Although the part of me that wanted to end it was very minor, the thought struck me that if Dave's suicidal nature somehow infected me, and the virus flared up, would I be able to fight off the fever? Especially with certain death only a few hundred yards away?

I stepped out of my cave at 6:30 p.m. Today was a cool day. It was probably only 100 degres instead of 120 or 130. The wind is blowing, and it's beautiful out. I'm still thinking of Dave—with a grieving but open heart. I stand and survey my surroundings. I feel God's presence.

"Are we having our conversation now?" I ask God. But I'm not actually asking—I'm sort of sarcastically commenting on the subtleness of, and lack of, God's communication. Just then, I feel the wind blow across my skin, and I feel *the Spirit* reach out to me from within the wind in an attempt to console me. But it's not enough—it's not even close.

It's 9:00 p.m., and as I'm eating my pita and olive oil, I hear Dave say, "Bill—isn't it great being here?"

"Yeah, it is," I reply. "It would be better if you were here too."

"But I am here, Bill," Dave says.

"You know what I mean," I say. "And don't give me any of that bull—you're here and you're not here."

"Okay—you're right," Dave says, feeling berated. "But, Bill," he says, "it got really . . ."

". . . crazy," I say, finishing his sentence. "I know, because you've told me that a hundred times already."

Dave could always dodge and run away from trouble whenever it came toward him. He used to enjoy riding by the Madison bike cops as they were stopped at red lights and yelling, "Get a real job!" Sometimes they chased him, but he was a triathlete with tree trunks for legs, so they never had a chance. Once they caught him, though, after a bike cop radioed ahead to a couple of Madison police in cop cars. They chased him down a dead-end street and trapped him.

"You should have seen the bike cop," Dave said, laughing. "When the Madison police asked him what I did, the bike cop said in this whiny voice, 'He went through a red light on his bike, and then told me to get a real job!'"

Dave got away with that one, but in the end running away got him killed. You see, if you try to run away too often—especially if the trouble is coming from inside you—you lose yourself and perhaps become mentally ill like Dave. If you run away from being mentally ill, you're as good as dead. And one day, a trouble he couldn't run away from came calling—and what was so odd about it was that he didn't do anything wrong. He was charged by the school and police with saying sexual things to sixth-grade girls and touching them. There were six girls who complained. Dave was freaked out by the whole thing and claimed he didn't do anything. But you know how the story goes—people believe the kids. A year later, the six girls confessed.

"We made it up because he made us stay after school one day for goofing around," they said, "and we were angry at him."

But it was too late, and Dave was never the same. He had been psychologically wounded by the incident, and conse-quently he stopped going out much and hardly socialized. He also became obsessed with two things. One was getting into physical therapy school, which I suppose was a reaction to the realization that as a teacher, he was always vulnerable to any future accusation a child may make.

The second was a hope he held on to that a long-distance relationship with a woman from New York would eventually work out.

These two things kept him going, but he also used them as a distraction so that he would not have to deal with the growing illness within him.

A verse in the Gospel of Thomas says, "If you bring forth what is within you—it will save you. If you don't bring forth what is within you—it will destroy you" (page 53, vs. 70).

Dave avoided what was deep within him, and it grew until it killed him. But Dave's is not a rare case. Many people destroy themselves by avoiding their inner spiritual lives. They don't die all at once, or as dramatically as Dave. Instead, they are the "walking dead," as Jesus called them; people who have traded away pieces of a real life in order to appease the unacknowledged dis-ease within them. You can see it in people—not by what they do, but by what they can't do. They look, but they can't see. They listen, but they can't hear. They talk to you but can't talk with you; they can't really talk with you about things that matter, like death, sadness, or love.

Two thousand years ago, Jesus said people had eyes but couldn't see, and had ears but couldn't hear (see Jeremiah 5:21). That's why I came to the desert, so that my eyes and ears could learn to see and hear.

day 11

I slept late this morning—till 6:15. As I looked out my tent, I saw a herd of five ibex (mountain goats that look like deer) walk past my tent not more than fifteen feet away. First, a large buck walked up and looked around, then the rest followed.

"That's a large male ibex leg," Tamir had said, referring to the two lower ibex legs I found in a cave on the sixth day.

"Probably was a wolf that killed it."

I can't help but wonder which one of the five ibex that walked by my tent this morning will find itself in the jaws of a wolf next. And why that one?

After my parents died, I lived with my sister. She was a great sister, but she wasn't my mother. She was busy with her three kids and a marriage that was falling apart.

Whenever I had been sick while my mother was alive, she made it special. She cooked me bacon and brought it to me along with 7UP as I lay on the couch watching television. She sat with me, rubbed my head, and said the kinds of things any mother would say to one of her sick children. But after my mother died, I moved in with my sister and lived in the basement. I remember the first time I was sick after my mother died. I lay in bed in the basement. My sister opened the basement door and asked, "Billy, do you need anything?"

"No," I said, and the basement door shut so swiftly that it sent out a wake of emptiness that washed over my sick body, leaving no doubt that things had changed.

Without direction in my life, I was lost, so I asked the most basic of questions: *What should I be? What should I do?*

I came up with what I now think was a simple and yet ingenious idea. Since adults had been around longer than me—a twelve-year-old boy—I figured they knew more. So I watched and observed them, and whatever they admired or wished to become, I reasoned, must be the highest ideal in the world—and that ideal is what I would try to become.

The highest ideal of Jesus's time was to be like the Sadducees and the Pharisees. They knew the Scriptures and were esteemed for it. They dressed well. They had money and power. Basically, they looked marvelous.

In our society, whom do we esteem and yearn to be like? Do we want to be like holy people? Or like movie stars? Do we dress more like holy people or movie stars? Do we buy cars more like those of holy people or movie stars? Do we try to look like holy people or movie stars?

In Jesus's time, everyone knew John the Baptist was a holy

person, but no one dressed in a hairy mantle like John the Baptist. Nobody, except a very few, tried to live as John the Baptist. Instead, most people emulated or sought to emulate the movie stars of Jesus's time—the Sadducees and Pharisees.

When Mother Teresa and Princess Diana died on the same day, who got more press coverage? Whom did people think of more? Whom would people rather be?

For the next nine years after my parents died, I tried to be like the people on television. They were all handsome and beautiful. All happy and charming. All had nice cars and houses. When I looked at the adults, I could see in their eyes that they wanted to be like TV people. If you doubt what I say, why was the "People" section of *Time* magazine found to be the most popular part of the magazine? Why do people dress or get haircuts like famous people? Why are celebrities paid a lot of money to endorse everything from cars to shoes?

No one ever paid Mother Teresa to endorse anything . . .

Finally, it was the oddest thing that brought down my house of cards. I started losing my hair at the age of nineteen, and so I couldn't be a movie star or the star of my own life any longer. I struggled to keep the show going for another few years, but eventually I just couldn't hide behind the perfect world I had created because it grew increasingly imperfect. And like the original human beings, Adam and Eve, I found myself naked and ashamed.

That's when Dave found my suicide notes.

"Are you going to kill yourself, Bill?" he asked. Of course I told him no, but actually I wasn't sure. I knew my life was over—I just wasn't sure how it would end.

"When will the end time come?" the disciples asked Jesus.

"The angels don't know, the Son doesn't know—only the Father knows," Jesus said (see Matthew 24:36; Mark 13:32).

The end for me came in the fall of 1981. I had been so depressed then that I had prayed for months for God to kill me. Each night as soon as my head hit the pillow, my prayers began.

"Please, God . . . ," I pleaded. "I know I'm only twenty-one years old, but I'm tired—I've had and seen enough of this life. Please, let me die. Please!"

But no matter how much I prayed, no matter how much I cried out during my nightly torture, and no matter how much I begged God to kill me, my prayers were never answered. What kind of God was this? When I prayed for a happy life, I was denied. And now when I prayed for death, I was denied again. What did God want from me? Why was I left in this hell—this place that was neither alive nor dead?

Since God wasn't killing me fast enough, I decided to kill myself. I had lately come to the realization that there was something in me that felt tight (as though it were holding on to life)—and this holding seemed to reside in my chest. Maybe if I could just let go of this grasping on to life, that would be enough to sever the cord that kept me attached to life. Thus my nightly attempts at ending my life began.

I would start by lying in bed and imagining myself as a

corpse. Then I would let go of my connection to my life systematically by letting go of my body, my emotions, and my thoughts. I thought if I could just disconnect from those three things, then perhaps my breathing would just stop and I would die. This detachment from my body, emotions, and thoughts was made even easier when I saw I had suffered because of possessing those three things.

After doing this "exercise" for months, one night I went deeper—actually, I shouldn't say I did it—*it just happened.* I went deeper than my body, my emotions, or my thoughts, and I found myself in a place where I was immersed in God. Immediately I realized that God had always been with me, though I hadn't been aware of it. I was filled with the knowledge that without a doubt, God had loved me, and had loved all of us, since the beginning—and even before the beginning, and throughout our lives. On that day I stood up and started a new life.

And that's why I went into the desert: to bring more of that place that is after death; that is after surrender and letting go; that is unconditional love—to bring more of that place into my life.

In the last months before Dave killed himself, I tried to get him to see a different psychiatrist and a different therapist. Dave had seen his present therapist off and on for eight years. I knew why Dave chose this therapist; Dave was smarter than him. The therapist never was able to get Dave to work on his core issues. What is even more disturbing to recall is that Dave's therapist actually got defensive and blocked my attempts when I suggested Dave see another psychiatrist.

"I'm a good therapist," he said anxiously. "You can ask any-one in town."

Dave blocked my help and the help of family and friends. He even pretended he was fine when we got him admitted to a psychiatric unit for nine days. Dave refused to sign the papers that waived his right to privacy—so he was able to get out on a Monday without any of his friends or family being told and killed himself a few days later.

Dave never had that mystical experience that would have saved him. Why me and not him?

Life is sometimes cruel, and what is most cruel is that each of us has to experience and *witness* its cruelty upon another. This cruelty is almost unforgivable. That's why I went into the desert—to forgive God for the life he's given me, for the life he's given people I know and love—and even for the life he's given those I have never known.

I seek to forgive.

As I look out through my mosquito net—out at the beautiful surroundings—I am not thinking of the desert's beauty. Instead, I feel grief and say, "I don't like this freakin' place."

I heard a lot of clucking in my cave, and when I looked up I saw two geckos. One ran over and bit the smaller one in the stomach. The smaller one opened its mouth, screeched, and ran away. The bigger one hissed at the other one and seemed to be saying, "I warned you that I'd kick your butt if I saw you around here."

It seems to me there are four levels on the spiritual path. At the first level, we don't care about spiritual things. At the second level, we become a seeker and ask questions. At the third level, we know what it means to be in God's presence because we've had the experience. At the fourth level, we stop identifying with being "someone who's in God's presence" because we've become God's presence. Not God himself, but "one with God," as Jesus said. What's funny is that level one and level four often look the same, because neither one asks about God.

I've gradually adopted some structure to my spiritual practices. First, I do forty-five minutes of sitting meditation and prayer at morning, noon, and night (which I will increase to one hour in ten days). Then I say the Jesus prayer throughout the day. I also do what I call "the prayer of clear awareness." It's a prayer of no words, a clear recognition that I am present to the present— and then a letting go of that recognition into "presence only."

It's getting dark and cool. I just took a long hike/walk in the desert. I usually stay close to a dirt road that runs through the desert, unless I'm within sight of certain landmarks. I've seen one four-wheel drive (within a half mile of my camp) since I've been here. I found what looked like an old wooden box that is now all busted up. I carried some of the wood back to camp and began making a fire. After I threw the wood on a pile of branches I had collected, I heard a short, shrill, animal scream. Then it was quiet. I imagined that a predator had just sneaked up on some unsuspecting prey, and just like that! Only time enough for one last scream.

In the desert, God can sneak up on you. In the cities and towns, people are so armored, so fearful of one another—even those they love—that God doesn't have a chance. Our guard is up. We're so skeptical. When we see God coming, we turn away as we might when we see a vacuum-cleaner or encyclopedia salesman coming and say, "Sorry, I'm not buying any today."

Or we stand waiting for God to do something different, something new.

"Show me your stuff," we say. "Show me something I haven't seen before."

God doesn't have anything new to show us. He's shown us everything. It's staring us in the face. That's what "We were made in God's image" means. We were shown the whole kit and caboodle, shown it in the very way we're made!

"But I don't see nuthin'!" you say. Well, I've got news for you. It isn't about what you see—it's about *who is doing the seeing*. Jesus said in the Gospel of Thomas, "The kingdom of heaven is spread out upon the earth, but men do not see it" (page 65, vs. 113). The world doesn't need to be changed by God or born again; it's our way of seeing that needs to be born again, and, more specifically, the seer needs to be born again.

"'What do you want me to do for you?' Jesus asked him. The blind man said, 'Rabbi, I want to see'" (Mark 10:51).

As I read and reread the Gospels, I am struck by the number of stories dealing with sight and blindness. The word *blind* is mentioned 46 times, and the word *see* is mentioned 162 times. That's because Jesus knew how hard it is to really see and how easy it is to make ourselves blind.

If you've ever asked "meaning of life" questions to someone who, let's say, watches *Wheel of Fortune*, then you'll get *the look*. You know what I mean; it's *the look* that drives crazy people crazy. It's *the look* that drives people to drugs. It's *the look* that forces people like me to travel around the world looking for someone who doesn't have *the look*. Because just about every person watches that show—and just about everybody has *the look*. Just recently, I realized to what extent we grow up in a world of *those looks*, those blank, glassy stares.

I was in a hospital waiting room while my older brother was being operated on. There were about thirty other people there reflecting deeply or talking softly about someone they cared about. The emotion was heavy, and even though most of the people weren't related, there was a sense of connection in the room. A sense of belonging because, at that moment, we all loved, and we all cared together. Sure, there was suffering in the room, but to be concerned and worried about those you love is a natural, sane suffering. This place felt real, and even though I saw pain in people, I sensed a deep connectedness and humanity. Thirty people who shared what it means to be alive and to care about people.

But then it happened. An old lady, perhaps seventy years old, got up and walked over to the television. In the middle of a sane, natural grieving process, she turned on *Wheel of Fortune*, and there it was. The heads of everyone slowly turned toward the television as though pulled by some invisible thread. I looked into the eyes of the people around me. The moment before, there had been life, but now nobody was there.

"Do you have eyes but fail to see . . . ?" Jesus asked (Mark 8:18).

Their eyes were vacant. Devoid of emotion. Devoid of presence. Devoid of life. They were the eyes of insanity. They were the eyes of people who turn on *Wheel of Fortune* while their loved ones might be dying on the operating table.

What angered me was that I had seen this look before. When I was twelve years old, I saw this look every time I asked people why my parents died. It's the glazed look that people give you as you pass them on the street or in a church.

In the hospital waiting room, I felt like I was sitting in the midst of a group trance, and then I realized, *This is where I've been my whole life. This is what I've battled my whole life—the* Wheel of Fortune *look*. Sometimes when I look in the mirror, I see that same glassy-eyed look in my eyes. Sometimes the mentally ill residents where I work cry, complain, and constantly ask for things. I want to tell them to leave me alone, but I don't. Instead, I find myself giving them *the look*—that same lifeless look that people gave me—and I'm a little afraid of being on my deathbed and realizing that I've never looked at anyone or anything. Because as long as you have eyes but fail to see, you're not really alive.

I mean, it's all right for a dead person to be dead, but if there's such a thing as a sin, it's being dead when you're still alive. It's not seeing with alive eyes. I think Jesus probably had that "real" look to him. That's why they killed him. Because if you're dead and you see someone who's alive, you get jealous and scared. You're reminded of what you're lacking. You want them dead, one way or another, just like you.

Children are born with that real look. They feel an aliveness in their hearts, and there's fire in their eyes. Children see—that's why Jesus said, "Be as little children" (see Matthew 18:3). Yet what example do we set for them when they look around and the norm is to be dead and blind?

As I walk back to camp, I am empty; there is no question in me—so there's no answer. But that isn't good enough for me (and that's a shame), so I start to call on God, and in the faintest, quietest whisper I hear the Presence that is present. My tears well up, and a voice says, "You don't need the trumpets or organs anymore to announce our relationship—our relationship is deeper than that. I am whispering to you now, but the time is coming when even that will stop. And then the real trust, the real knowing will be that you and I are indivisibly connected. If you think of me, then there will be you thinking of me.

"But if you rest all that activity, we will be what we have always been—together as One. When you look, I will also be looking. When you eat, I will also be eating. And when you laugh or cry, I will also be laughing or crying. But if you should ever doubt, then I will be there—but apart from you—in order to comfort you. But when you don't doubt, I will be as you."

As the internal voice stopped, I became afraid. For so long I had depended on the God who is apart from me. I turned to that God. Depended on that God to answer my questions. But if the questions ceased, could I go without the comfort of those answers?

When Adam and Eve ate from the Tree of Knowledge of Good and Evil, they started a chain of events that led to their loss of Eden. They were caught in their thinking about Good or Evil, this or that, question or answer—opposites or separateness. If they could have stopped the thinking that spun out of control or, better yet, stopped believing the thoughts they were thinking, would they have found that they were standing square in the center of the Garden of Eden—never having left?

day 12

I'm bored today, although I saw two hikers with big back-packs stop to make a meal about three hundred yards from me on an adjacent cliff. I knew they were about three hundred yards away because I play golf, and I figured with a good drive, I'd hit them.

They sounded like they were speaking Hebrew. They were singing—and laughed occasionally. They looked rugged—and knew they looked rugged. They stood on the edge of the cliff, surveyed the landscape, and seemed pleased with themselves until one of them saw me. He pointed at me, and his body was shaking as he stammered something in Hebrew.

"It took us days of walking through the desert to get here," I imagined him saying, "and there's some guy in a mosquito net over there!"

Alone, my thoughts turn to women. Specifically, past lovers. I can't help remembering the closeness of bodies, the light perspiration on the skin, and . . . I'm stopping right there. Let's just say that since I've been in the desert, I've gone over what's possible between a man and a woman. I try to catch myself and let the memories go—so as not to torture myself. But is it really torture to remember them? I'm not sure, but if I promote those kinds of memories while I'm here, they will preoccupy my mind.

But I will tell you that on the fourth day, when I walked into the hostel for my mosquito net, I saw two women—about five hundred yards away—and I could smell their perfume.

"Your senses get stronger in the desert," Tamir had told me.

Lust. I can remember very clearly the day the priest read in church this passage: "Anyone who looks at a woman lustfully has already committed adultery with her in his heart" (Matthew 5:28).

I was sitting in the third row, and I must have been in about fourth grade. I remember thinking, *No one can do that*. No one can control the desire he feels for a woman—his behavior, yes; but what seems to come of its own—lust, no. It can't be controlled. I don't really know why I thought that back then, because in the fourth grade I don't think I even knew what it meant to desire a woman—but I knew Jesus was asking too much. Since then, I've learned that scholars question whether Jesus ever said it, or what he meant by it. I think everyone has to admit that the church's view of sex is a little skewed. Paul said it's better for people not to have sex—but to get married if they have to. It's too bad the Bible doesn't talk about how great or beautiful sex is. It seems any sexual person in the New Testament is in danger of being stoned.

I dreamed last night of a man who was holding his newborn baby. I heard the baby cry, and when I looked, I could tell he was hurting it on purpose. Then he walked a bit, and the baby cried again. He was squeezing the baby, almost folding it in half.

"Are you hurting that baby on purpose?" I asked.

"Yes, I am," he said with such childlike honesty that I knew he was mentally ill—and that he would keep hurting the baby. I dropped to my knees and wept so deeply that my body was shuddering. Both he and another man turned and watched me cry.

I'm bored—yet I've got twenty-eight days left. I say my prayers, but they lack fire. Maybe I'll just allow myself to be bored and see what happens.

If I had a television right now, I'd turn it on.

Now I'm thinking all kinds of things, like whatever happened to the rock group Steppenwolf? They had a great album and so much potential.

The idea I had the other day is working great. I used my dinner bowl as a substitute shovel, carried sand to my cave, and filled the spaces between the boulders. It leveled out the floor of the cave so that I can lie and sit comfortably—actually, it's about as comfortable as lying on a flat rock, but it is luxurious compared to what I had before. Almost every night the wind blows at 20 to 30 mph. In order to keep the wind from blowing away all the sand I carried into my cave (my cave only has one and a half walls), I laid a tarp down over the sand and duct-taped it to the surrounding rocks. My living space is now about six feet by two and a half feet by three feet. It's sort of like being in a small jail cell—but the difference is, I've chosen it freely.

day 13

The foxes were barking very close to my tent last night.

I woke up angry, in a bad mood, and I wanted to stay in bed. I filled my water bottles with resentful movements. Despite my anger, I did catch a fly in my hand and let an ant crawl on a piece of paper and then put both outside my tent.

I walked to my cave, thinking about people who say how great life is all the time. Sure, life is great a lot of the time—but it's also horrible. And *we never asked for this*. In my first book, *Tying Rocks to Clouds*, I was surprised at how many of the wise people I interviewed said, "You know, it's been nice, but I really don't want to come back again."

Hearing that allowed me to admit I didn't really want to come back either. Previously, I had convinced myself I did, because I thought that wise, enlightened people loved life all the time, that they were happy all the time. But I've met many of them—and evidently they are not.

On the thirteenth day, everything stopped. It seemed hot, with very little wind. I walked down to the edge at 4:00 p.m. (which I do almost every day because at 4:00 p.m. the edge is in the shade) and sat on my rock. It was a rectangular rock with the bottom left corner missing. I placed another rock under it and propped it up so that its seat was pretty flat. My butt has been hurting today. Maybe it finally got tired of sleeping and sitting on rock all day. Even on my rock down by the edge, my butt hurt. Even the best of the rocks around here aren't very comfortable. Maybe I can handle it for a few hours or a few days— or even a week—but after a week, my behind said, "Enough! I understand you have this 'manly' need to sit on a rock, but it's pushing two weeks, and I've had enough!"

So this got me thinking *lawn chair* again. The stupidest thing I did was leave my cot and camping chair at home. What a stupid I am! I could kick myself. But at the last minute I was afraid the airline would charge me an extra seventy dollars for a third piece of luggage. So I left the cot and the camping chair I bought. I figured I'd have time to get a similar chair in Israel, but then Tamir and I left for the desert the morning after I got here. But who am I kidding? Tamir was ready to have me sleep in the cave or outside—under the stars the whole forty days. He would have been shocked if I had suggested a lawn chair.

But as I sat on my rock, my pained behind was actually able to convince my brain that a lawn chair was a good idea.

"Brain," my rear end said, "Bill will sit on this lawn chair and his body will relax. Then he will start meditating twice as much—in his lawn chair *and* in his cave!

"Enduring pain is not conducive to meditation," it added, "and besides, Jesus sat on hard surfaces most of his life—*he was used to it*. While my friend Bill here—he has a skinny little butt—there's not a lot of flesh between the rock and bone."

Anyway, the point I was trying to make is that *everything stopped today*. I'm bored—low in excitable energy. The hype of being here is kaput. My mind no longer wants to rouse energy in order to entertain or add to what is happening. So I'm bored—and when I let go of my thoughts of "being bored," there's stillness. Incredible and simple stillness.

day 14

Nothing washes away the old pain of this world like a good cry.

Nothing clears the eyes, makes the blind see, like a good cry.

Nothing softens a man's heart so that his ears will be opened like a good cry.

I decided to bow this morning—in part to pray and in part to exercise the colon and get it moving. I immediately felt myself in God's presence, before God in a very clear way.

"Please, God, help me make the best use of this time," I prayed. "Help it be of use to others. Help me know the best way to prepare myself, to be what it is I should, to be the way that is best.

"Do I just lie here and allow myself to naturally open to you even as my thoughts and feelings sometimes wander off to other things? Or do I take a stronger stance—use my will to sit straight-backed as I work more while I'm in your presence?"

"Bill," the voice came back. "I'm very happy with what you've done. I love you. Look at me—look up at me; raise your head and look at me."

As I looked up, the face of God looked back at me directly in front of my face.

"I love you."

My face looked down—ashamed to be told that.

"Look at me!" the voice said strongly.

"Look up at me," the voice said again—this time tenderly.

I looked up with an undeserving feeling in my heart. Then *Hands of Spirit* placed themselves on each side of my head and held me there while I heard the words "I love you" over and over again until my resistance—the fear and hardness of my heart—gave way; the veil that separated love from myself also dropping away, revealing a clear path from God's love to my heart.

I wept, and the trumpets of my tears toppled the walls that had enclosed and hidden away my secrets and my shame.

"I'm afraid that I'm doing it wrong."

"I love you—and everything you've done, I'm happy with."

"But I've done some things . . ."

"I love you, Bill, and you are a good man who's done his best—you learn from your mistakes. And mistakes? The world is full of mistakes! It's built on mistakes. You know those places—when you climb a mountain—those places where you put your feet or your hands and then pull and push yourself up?"

"Those places are mistakes. You get up the mountain through mistakes."

I was freed by the simple fact that the Spirit of God prefaced anything it said to me with the living experience of "I love you . . ."

As this love enveloped me, my soul relaxed into its spiritual comfort. And as I sank deeper into the soul by way of weeping, I could see my parents with the Spirit—*they were Spirit*. My heart gently asked if they, my parents, approved of me. Within the abundance of Spirit, they said they loved me. And they started to cheer me on.

"Go get 'em. We're proud of you," they said, clapping as though I had just scored a 10 on the balance beam in the Olympics. Their support was so over the top that it was funny.

My mom held me as my father patted me on the shoulder.

"I love you so much," she said. Her love was always easy to feel.

"I love you too," my father said a bit more stiffly—but I could tell it was an absolute feeling frenzy for him.

"No hard feelings?" he asked.

When soul meets soul so thoroughly and deeply that it experiences only itself, there is instantaneous forgiveness. Actually, the grudges themselves dissolve, which leaves only soul and its essence—*which is forgiveness*. When Jesus forgave sins or gave us the ability to forgive sins, *he was only affirming what is already true in the depths of our souls.*

"No hard feelings," I said to my father.

My father smiled and looked down for a moment, at which time I took the opportunity to poke him in his big, fat, Buddha-looking belly.

"Hey!" he said, reacting with pleasure that I had gotten him back.

I wept some more as what had been outside became even more within, and what had been within became even more without.

How strange it is to realize that nothing needs to be done to experience God's presence. *We are extensions of his presence,* so much so that if God ceased to be present, we'd cease. Don't get me started on these crazy theological arguments, like, If we cease our ego—which separates us from God—then is there only God? And if there is only God and no one separate from God to say, "Hey, look, there's God," does the concept of God cease? And then there is only . . . ? Like I said, don't get me started.

I met a young man with a ponytail who worked at a coffee shop down south. He told me that he had studied in the Middle East for a year.

"I studied Islam," he said.

"Oh. Then do you think Christianity and Islam worship the same God?" I asked.

"Of course not," he said. "They worship different gods."

I often wonder, when someone says they study something, what do they mean? Do they mean they read books about it? Do they mean they watch it from afar?

I believe Jesus went into the desert because he was tired of hearing about God from others and then asking them questions (as he did in the temple as a boy). He was tired of reading about God. He was especially tired of watching other people bow and pray to God. I believe he went into the desert because he had "married" God while being baptized by John. His forty days in the desert comprised his metaphorical wedding night with his beloved. During those nights and days, he grew to know his beloved, his God, in the way that two devoted lovers would know each other through seven lifetimes of wedding nights.

The Israeli fighter jets are flying over more than usual. I hope it doesn't mean anything.

When Tamir visited last week, Ya'el came with him. Ya'el mainly sat on the edge of the cliff, while Tamir and I talked about supplies and wildlife.

"See how this snake has two markings on the back of its head? They look like eyes so that a bird of prey flying overhead thinks that the snake is watching it—when it's not."

I liked Tamir and his desert lectures. But I must admit I had to make a concerted effort to focus on him while Ya'el was sitting on the edge of the cliff looking attractive, fiery, and sensual—and barefoot—which only added to her sensuality. Tamir and I wore sandals, but she engaged the sharp stones and boulders with a soft, pliable foot. She wanted to feel her body against Mother Earth, even if it was a bit uncomfortable at times. She had left an ultraconservative Jewish religious group only years before, where she had to dress plainly and wear a scarf on her head whenever she went outside. But now on this day, while visiting a man alone in the desert with his thoughts, feelings, and desires, she wore a short top that revealed her belly button.

Like I said, I made the conscious effort to focus on Tamir more than Ya'el. I liked her and her wisdom, but I didn't want things getting weird. When Tamir and Ya'el were about to leave, he stood behind her, wrapped both arms around her, and held her against himself as he faced me.

"I won't be coming next week with your water," he said. "It will either be Yusuf the Bedouin or . . . this beautiful woman."

I looked at Ya'el and then back at Tamir—then at both of them.

"How will I be able to tell which one is which?" I asked in feigned ignorance.

We all laughed.

What men have done to women is horrible. We desire them—with a passion often uncontrollable. We then are so afraid and hateful of our "out-of-control" desire that we project that, put that on women. We make them put a veil over their bodies in order to hide their curves. We make Eve be the temptress in the Garden of Eden. Do you remember what Adam told God when he stuttered and stumbled for an excuse?

"Er . . . uh . . . the woman you put here with me," Adam said, "*she* gave me some fruit from the tree and I ate it" (see Genesis 3:12).

I remember seeing the outline of a fox—the silhouette as it moved along in the darkness—by the light of the moon. I can't remember if this was part of a dream or real.

Fifteen minutes into my meditation, I hear a "clucking" followed by hissing sounds. This is usually the sound the geckos in my cave make when they are getting ready to fight. I look up and see two geckos. One is stalking the other (who is obviously trying to avoid a fight); but the one who is trying to avoid the confrontation never really or entirely runs away. Instead, he stays within ten feet of his pursuer and then hisses and raises his tail in a crooked manner. Then they stare at each other.

Every fifteen minutes or so, I open my eyes to see if they are still staring at each other, and they are. Neither one moves. And I hear locusts in the background, whose constant noise reminds me of the background music in a cowboy movie like *High Noon*. It adds drama and tension to the gecko duel.

When my meditation is almost done, I hear the aggressive clucking and look up to see one gecko hopping across the twelve-inch space between two pillars in order to chase the other one down. He lands on the other side like Spider-Man, and before he can climb around the corner of the last boulder separating him from his foe, his foe scampers away around a corner. When the aggressive gecko turns the corner, he finds the object of his aggression gone.

In the fourth century the deserts of the Middle East were populated by monks who had fled city life. They went into the desert to understand and experience God—not in and through the words of someone else or even through the Scriptures—but through a direct meeting.

What had begun as an experience of God regressed into what Jesus railed against—laws and penalties. As Thomas Merton pointed out in *The Wisdom of the Desert*, "Three whips hung from a palm tree outside the church of Scete: one to punish delinquent monks, one to punish thieves, and one for vagrants."

Jesus came to set us free in love, not to imprison us in more doctrines and rules. Too often I see his teachings and words used to whip, abuse, and judge those who do not subscribe to a particular church doctrine. But as Saint Anthony said, "Whatever you see your soul to desire according to God, do that thing, and you shall keep your heart safe."

To see what one's soul desires, one has to go beyond any doctrine or social pressure. One has to go even beyond oneself.

How do I think I do God's will? How do I know what God's will is?

Listen.

Become an ear to God's voice.

That's why I came to the desert. So that I could learn to listen again. Life is so fast-paced in the world, doing this, doing that—saying this, saying that. If I just stop for a while, I will start to quiet down and hear something other than my own thoughts. I hear God's voice; actually, I feel God's voice and turn it into words. Which is only appropriate when you realize the human ear "hears" nothing—it "feels" sound with its various vibrating membranes and bones and turns it into hearing.

But I also feel or hear my own deep desires, so how do I know or tell the difference between my desires and God's?

Well, sometimes they're the same, and at other times they are not. I do my best to discriminate. Sometimes I act on my desire and think it's God's desire. Then afterward, it appears that I was mistaken. But in that way, I keep attuning myself, finding out which chord is true and which is false. Only by mistaking one's own desires for God's countless times can true discrimination of God's voice come. But most people seem to not want to struggle with hearing God's voice. They want it easier, cleaner. They want a list of ten things to do.

So, they think, *if I do these ten things, I'm okay—right?*

Depends.

Once upon a time there was a man who tried to drink ice— he choked and then died of thirst. Another man held the ice against his heart until it melted into a glass. He then drank the living water that had once been cold and hard.

Every once in a while when I'm doing something, I swear I can hear Tibetan monks singing or symbols crashing together as if there is a celebration somewhere. Whenever I stop to listen, there is only silence.

"The bedouins call you Jesus," Ya'el said. She was dropping off my weekly supply of water. "They ask me, 'How is Jesus doing?'"

The amazing thing about Ya'el's arrival was that I smelled her coming. I was meditating when all of a sudden I smelled a very pleasant perfume smell—it had to be Ya'el. A couple of minutes later, I heard "Hello?" as she called to me from above the cave.

We talked for a few minutes, and then she told me that she had relationship problems. I listened and didn't say much, as I wasn't going to get involved in *that one*. Ya'el mentioned her tendency to act "fiery" almost as a way to stay out of the "nothingness" she'd been feeling the last few weeks.

"That's why I came to the desert," I said. "To die into that nothingness—to quit trying to prop myself up artificially through some kind of personality manipulation."

"When you're around people, they want you to 'be up,'" I said. "There's too much social pressure preventing you from dying. That's why I'm here alone. So no one can keep me from dying."

As I said, Ya'el wore perfume today. She also wore shorts and has nice legs.

Ya'el is also a tough woman. There's not a lot of extra butter on the bread—if you know what I mean. Things I consider an added comfort, she considers a luxury. I mentioned that my bottom was hurting and I wanted an air mattress.

"What about the air mattress we got you?" she asked, referring to an air mattress so big and thick that I called it "the Hindenburg."

"It's not self-inflating," I said.

"Oh," she said, "that's why it was so cheap.

"Pretty soon," she added, "you will have so much stuff out here you will have to build a house."

After she said that, I decided not to mention the lawn chair.

Both Jesus and the Buddha were tempted three times. One of the Buddha's temptations was a beautiful woman, but none of Jesus's three temptations during his forty days in the desert involved a woman.

day 15

Last night something was scratching at one of the plastic washbasins outside my tent. Whenever I flashed my flashlight through the screened flap, the scratching stopped. Then a few minutes later it started up again. This went on for nearly an hour. It dawned on me that something had crawled into the tub and couldn't get out. I was already naked and lying on my bed. I did not want to get up, especially with the mosquitoes looking for a snack.

"Hey you," I said through the flap, "if you're still there in the morning, I'll let you out."

The next morning the tub was empty.

I'm lying in my mosquito net. I don't want to meditate. *Real* meditation creates awareness of yourself—it deepens awareness through a "seeing" then a "relaxing into" what you're seeing. But I'm not in the mood to see today. I don't want to see what I've been avoiding. It would be easier to eat a nice fattening meal right now: potatoes, eggs, a few pancakes, and coffee. Yes, that's it. I wish I could drench all that stuff just below the surface of my psyche in fat and heavy food. That usually works. And then a cup or two of coffee to hype me up so much that I vibrate at a different rate than the things I want to avoid. But I don't have any of that here—nor do I have a television, a newspaper, a woman, or well-meaning friends to distract me. Instead, I just lie in a bed so deep and boring that instead of "the kingdom of God," I have "the boredom of Bill."

I have a dilemma. There's a wasp building a house not more than a foot away from my net.

"Go use that house over there," I say, referring to a little clay wasp house already built another ten feet away.

Anyway, I can't decide if I should destroy his house as he's building it so that he will be discouraged and build somewhere else or if I should let him live here. Maybe I should learn to live with him? Nah—it's better to destroy the beginnings of his house now and avoid trouble later.

I knocked down the foundation of the wasp's house. I haven't seen him for a while.

I came to the desert to die, to dismantle, to surrender who I think I am—and be regenerated. Reborn. Born again. Start over. I don't know about you, but I can tell when I need to die. Usually, my heart becomes enclosed, my thoughts start to wander, and I already feel a bit deadened. Jesus called these people (or us) "the spiritually dead" (Luke 9:59 NLT). The spiritually dead aren't necessarily boring people or boring to look at. Often they're the ones making the most noise, laughing the most, telling you how good they've got it. But they're already dying. You can see it in their eyes—they lack sustained presence. Or in their touch—they lack tender vulnerability. Often they create a life that is trying to convince themselves and others they aren't dying and they aren't dead.

I went to the desert to die with dignity so that I could live with dignity. Dying is actually just another way to cry. They both cleanse the eyes and the soul.

Thirty-five minutes into my second meditation, I look at the clock. "Ten minutes left?" It has seemed like forever. I look at the clock's second hand to make sure it is working. It's moving so slowly—each second is like a day. I bow my head at the end and cry a bit.

"I don't know if I can do this," I say in God's presence.

"Then don't," replies the Spirit.

"You mean I don't have to do this?" I ask, looking for any hint of disapproval.

"If you stay, I will love you," the Spirit of God says, "and if you leave, I will love you."

"Then why am I here?"

"You tell me."

"But I felt called."

"You were."

I looked to Jesus and wondered if I was playing some game with myself.

"Was I called by you?"

"By us," Jesus, smiling.

"Us?"

And as I gaze onto Jesus, I am enveloped by a clear light.

"I'm afraid," I say after a few moments.

"I know," Jesus, "but it will come—it will come."

I try to live my life like Jesus. Not that I am trying to do the things he did: to be crucified or be a preacher or die a virgin. I try to live my life like Jesus in that *he was who Jesus was meant to be*. Just as I want to be *who Bill was meant to be*. As the old Jewish-Christian story goes (sort of), I'm not afraid that when I die God will ask me, "Why weren't you a Jesus, Moses, or Abraham?" No, I'm afraid that God will ask me, "Bill—why weren't you what Bill was meant to be?"

Jesus Christ—*Christ* is Greek and means "anointed one." It came from the Jewish idea that God anoints certain people to carry out a purpose. For example, King David is "anointed" by God, and David refers to Saul as "the Lord's anointed." The priest is also anointed in Leviticus 4:3.

Jesus was special not because he was anointed by God, but because he was anointed by God and *knew it*. Actually, we are all anointed by God to do something special and something unique. You can't be born without being anointed. To be like Jesus, all we need to do is be anointed (which we are) and then—*know it*.

The wasp returned and started rebuilding his house. When he went away, I knocked it down again. But I think he'll keep trying to build it, so I put three large rocks over the place where he tried to build.

He returned and buzzed around those rocks for twenty minutes trying to find a way to build his house there.

In my life I've tried to build things where they weren't meant to be. Whether it was building competition between friends or continuing to build a love relationship after it had ended or building a self-centeredness in the midst of my soul.

I came to the desert in order to allow the things I've built to be knocked down.

It was still so hot in my tent at 8:00 p.m. that I went and lay in my cave till 9:00 p.m. I looked up at the stars.

"Can you believe I'm in a freakin' cave at night in the Judean desert?" I said out loud.

I finally got up and left the cave after something crawled over me. Since it was dark, I couldn't see what it was.

Before I got into my tent, I decided to retrieve a bottle that was lying by some rocks. I was wearing my head flashlight, and good thing I was, because I almost stepped on what looked like a rock—but it turned out to be a coiled-up snake.

I woke up to the sound of a dirt bike, its engine whining in the distance.

I also woke up to five red ants in my tent. I killed them right then and there. There were others outside my tent, trying to get in using the same route the others took. Where my flap zips closed, there is maybe an eighth-inch opening where the horizontal and vertical zippers meet. I have to be really careful, because it would be a disaster if a bunch of them found their way into my tent and into my food.

After Jesus healed, fed, and loved people in the Gospel of Mark, he proclaimed, "I am a Human Being." He referred to himself as the "Son of Man" more than eighty-one times, which was an ancient way of saying "son of a human being" or "a human being." Many people would scoff at this and say, "Jesus was more than human." I agree; Jesus was more than human. He was a human *being*. And that's why I came to the desert; because I was only human—I wasn't a human *being* yet.

Jesus said he was the "Son of God," and he implied that we were God's children when he said, "I am returning to my Father and your Father" (John 20:17). He didn't say he was returning "to my Father and your Stepfather" or "to my Father and your future Father." He was saying we were already God's sons and daughters. How could God adopt us at some future time (as some theologians believe) when we were already God's children by right of birth?

I meditated the first thing this morning. I wanted to rest in Being a bit before I started thinking so much. Maybe if my thoughts begin with the experience of Being—with the experience of God's presence—my thoughts and emotions will serve my day from a place of Being—from the feet of God.

And then I can rightfully be called a "human being."

I went to the edge and sat down while doing the "Lord, have mercy" prayer. I was using my Indian beads that Mother Teresa and the Dalai Lama had blessed. I sat a few feet away from the edge—on the rocky, gray, smooth limestone. I gave myself some room for error in case I tripped and fell forward— I would have space to recover. As I did my Jesus prayer and looked at the "fall" off the edge, it felt an awful lot like eternity. It still scared me, though, as I felt the fear collecting in my tensing stomach, my chest and back becoming more rigid.

I suddenly had flashes of jumping. It scared me. The visions were spontaneous, and I was afraid I would act spontaneously. I tried to relax, to "feel" the feeling and let it pass. But what if the feeling overwhelmed me and compelled me to act?

I said the Lord's Prayer some more. How easy it would be to end it all here. To end any chance of suffering in the future. I could feel a part of me soften and release itself at the thought of ending my suffering. I could actually "see" that part of me—it looked like the bark of an old tree: deeply etched, weather-beaten, and gnarled. This bark, whether by seeing or by running one's fingertips across the textured depths, told a story—a story of life and survival, of struggle and deep suffering. If I jumped, this story would be over—gone—like a page torn from a book and tossed away. And that would be it. *Suffering* and *jumping* had made their case, and it was a pretty good case.

Now it was life's turn. It had me reexperience and feel all the joy, fun, and happy faces I had come across in my life, together with all the unexpected surprises that had lit up my soul. If I jumped, they would be gone, and all the future joys and surprises would also be gone—*and missed*.

I weighed the two against each other: the experience of life with its joy and suffering versus death and the end of suffering.

"There will be plenty of time to be dead," my friend Steve always said to his suicidal clients.

And there's not much time to live, I thought.

I paused—took it all in. *Yes*, I decided. I would deal with the suffering of life—put up with it, so that I could experience the other things life offers.

I made the choice.

I said the Lord's Prayer some more, and then Jesus's presence became known.

"Why don't I jump?" I asked.

"Look at me," Jesus said.

I looked at him, and then he said again, "Look at me."

It was then that I realized my chest had been rigid and that my rigidity had blinded my heart, so much so that even though I had been looking, *I wasn't seeing*.

I exhaled, and my heart opened like a flower. I felt love—and that's why I didn't jump—because I had felt love and loved. And that's why my friend Dave killed himself—he had lost the ability to feel loved.

"I'm sorry, Bill," Dave had said to me in the back of the police car on the way to the psych unit. He had said it with such a deep sincerity and care *for me* that I thought he felt bad because he was putting me through the hassle of getting the police involved and admitting him to the hospital.

"It's okay," I said.

"I'm sorry, Bill," Dave said again.

"Dave, it's all right," I said, and then it hit me. *He's apologizing for something else, and I don't know what it is.*

Twelve days later he was dead, and then I knew; Dave was apologizing because he knew his life was over. He was at the edge, and he knew he was going to jump. Dave wasn't apologizing so much for killing himself; no, that wasn't it. Dave was apologizing because we were friends—not the kind of friends who drink together, play golf together, or complain about their wives together . . . We were more than that. Dave and I had seen into each other's souls, and if you ever do that with another human being, then you know there is an unspoken contract that is automatically made. It goes something like this: No matter what happens to either of us, we will be there for the other till the end. We will remind each other of *that thing* we see in, and experience with, each other *but that can never be said.*

I'm not being coy when I say this, but if you don't know what *that thing* is—well, I can't tell you. All I can say is that when you see it in another person, you relax. You relax because you know that you are not alone in your knowing or your wakefulness.

"You know," Dave used to say, "some kids at my school are aliens. You would know which ones if you met them."

"And they know you know," he'd continue, "but you can't say anything . . . because then *the knowing* that you both share would disappear—and the situation would be awkward."

Of course Dave wasn't talking about aliens from outer space—he was talking about the alienation of seeing in a blind world; about being spiritually awake in a sleeping world. So Dave was apologizing for breaking the contract of *knowing with another.* He knew he was at the edge of himself and would be leaving me with one less person to share *the secret of knowing* with.

Jesus also found himself at the edge. That was one of his temptations.

"If you are the Son of God," the devil said after taking Jesus to the pinnacle of the temple, "then jump off . . ."

"Why am I afraid of jumping?" I asked Jesus as I got up from the edge and started walking back to my cave.

"Because you know what deep suffering is," he said.

And as he said that, a sharp, piercing chill ran through me from head to foot and stopped me in my tracks. I turned to the side and placed my arms on a stone ledge. Then I bowed my head and wept.

How true! How true! my tears said. If I were to jump, I would be immersed in and feel all the pain that I had sought to avoid.

First I cried for Dave's death and suffering. Then the others came—my parents, my brother, my friends—all those who had died. Their memories came, the impact of their lives and deaths upon me; suffering, only made worse by the joy we had together, slowly filtered through my body and soul.

With the stones, boulders, and sands witnessing, I wept.

10:00 P.M.

I'm as happy as a clam. It was cool today. Only 100 degrees. It was windy tonight, so I was able to go for a nice walk. I usually just wear my shorts and sandals these days when walking about. In my mosquito net, I'm naked—as naked as Adam and Eve realized they were after they ate from the Tree of Knowledge. Of course, I'm trying to correct their major mistake, which was judging themselves so harshly once they realized they were naked. They were ashamed of being naked, and that's why they hid from God. Now of course the Bible isn't talking physical nakedness. It's talking about spiritual nakedness. There is something in Adam and Eve, and even in us, that doesn't want to be spiritually naked. It doesn't want to be seen or to see—too much. Jesus was spiritually naked and didn't hide from God. If Jesus taught anything, it was to be spiritually and soulfully naked before God. I think that's what "to love God with your whole heart and soul" means. If you're busy loving God—giving it everything you have and not holding anything back or covering yourself up in God's presence—then you're naked in your love, and self-judgment and the tendency to hide don't have a chance.

I'm running out of supplies—actually, I have plenty of the food I hate, but the good stuff I'm using up. I don't like starting fires out here or even starting the stove, so I've been eating things I don't have to cook: cashews, almonds, dried fruit, pita bread with olive oil, and Clif Bars. I brought twenty-five Clif Bars with me. They're a tasty, hearty energy bar. But I'm just about out, and I'm only sixteen days into my forty.

I brought a lot of noodles and oatmeal. The oatmeal is too hot to eat in the morning and a pain to clean up, so I've been eating rice noodles. But they are made from white rice, and they're beginning to taste like paste.

While lying in my tent, I ate the last Clif Bar, a chocolate one, together with a cup of dry soy milk. It wasn't great—but here in the desert it felt like a feast.

"Bartender," I said, lifting up my cup, "I'll have another soy milk!"

Then, turning to my fellow bar patrons, I said, "And one for everyone in the house! The dry soy milk's on me!"

day 17

J esus amazed and shocked people because he would teach
them on his own authority, unlike the scholars (see Matthew
7:29 NLT).

Where did Jesus get this authority? In the only place
"authority of the soul" can ever be found—*in the soul*. Jesus went
out into the desert to grovel, cry, laugh, and "joy" himself back
into, more deeply into, his soul. But first he had to battle the
demons—the temptations of Satan.

On the way to the city of Caesarea Philippi, Jesus called Peter
"Satan" (see Matthew 16:23). Why did Jesus do that? Especially
since Peter was just trying to be helpful? It was because Peter was
opposing Jesus's deeper sense of destiny and Jesus's deeper sense
of God's will. *Satan* comes from the Hebrew word for "opposer"
or "adversary." And that's the point: we each have friends, and
even parts of ourselves, that are often opposed to our deeper truth
and connection with God. Even though they are trying to be

helpful, they are still adversaries. So how do we find the skill and the courage to rebuff those well-meaning adversaries—especially when they love us and have often loved us in the past?

I've been watching bugs a lot more since I've been here. It's like having the Discovery Channel on twenty-four hours a day. And I have so many questions. For example, why do bees and wasps land on the sand and dig little holes like a cat in a litter box?

Why does the gecko lick his own butt? Actually, Tamir told me the answer to this during one of his later visits. "There is not much water in the desert," he said, "so the gecko licks up its own urine and reuses it."

And the large black beetle—what a slow-footed and ancient-looking bug he is. He moves so slowly that I'm sure whatever he's going after is long gone by the time he gets there—eaten up by other bugs. But I've watched this guy closely, and he's taught me things. He has six legs—three on each side—and his back legs are very long. I watched him for forty-five minutes as he tried to climb over a large boulder. What he does first is move his right arm (very quickly) up and down across the face of a rock. It looks like he's scratching the back of the rock. He does this until his right claw catches in a small, almost imperceptible crack to lift himself up by. Then he does the same with the left arm until he finds a stable footing. Then his back four legs follow, except for his back right leg—the longest leg. He leaves that hanging, just in case he starts to fall; then he uses it to try to bolster himself up. I watched him climb almost all the way up a boulder. He expended a huge amount of energy, and

I was so taken up by his heroic and persistent effort that I let out a loud groan when he fell only inches from the top.

He landed on his back and then wobbled back and forth until he was able to roll onto his feet again. Then he began climbing the boulder once again. But I couldn't bear to watch, because if he were to fall again when so close to the top, I thought I would die from disappointment.

I want to go home now.

I'm tired of getting bitten by bugs. I'm tired of being beaten and controlled by the sun. I'm tired of never quite being as comfortable as when I'm at home. I'm tired of being aware of myself.

While lying under my net, I looked at my hands and arms. I inspected them. They looked old—starting to wrinkle. It was just two weeks before my forty-second birthday. My mortality was staring me in the face. The flies buzzed about.

"*Bzzzz, bzzzz,*" a fly said, "*bzzzz, bzzz*—you die—*bzzzz, bzzzz, bzzzz.*"

I lifted up the net and looked at the brown rocky canyon against the bluest of skies. Life here was beautiful and majestic, but it was also barren, ruthless, and unforgiving.

That was the desert.

When I spilled water onto the sand, it actually sounded like Rice Krispies. The ground was so hot that it sizzled.

I sat for nearly an hour today. There was so much energy in my meditation that my teeth were chattering.

If the kingdom of heaven is within, as Jesus said, why don't we experience it?

Three reasons: thoughts, emotions, and the body.

I know many people who are very intelligent. They are great lawyers, writers, doctors. They have a good grasp of thinking, of logic; they know how to think—but they are caught within the corral of thoughts.

I know many people whose emotions were blocked, and they worked on these hardened, rigid emotions in therapy until they were free within their emotions—able to express them freely. But they were still caught within the corral of emotion. Their pasture was much bigger now—but it was still fenced in.

And the body? I know many people who work with the body: exercise it, run, do yoga. They deal with the energy of the body—it's rigidifying anxiety and tension. They are freer in the body—*but still trapped by the body*.

The kingdom of heaven is not limited to any one of those three things, though the kingdom of heaven flows freely through them and thus can occasionally be experienced within them. But ultimately, the kingdom of heaven is free—free to roam within them and outside them. Actually, thoughts, emotions, and bodily sensations are three things that take place within the vast being of the kingdom of heaven, and thus to grasp on to any one of the three is to divide the kingdom—and Jesus said, "A house divided against itself cannot stand" (see Matthew 12:25).

Jesus's presence is growing stronger. Increasingly, whenever I ask Jesus or God a question, the answer is that first I am allowed to see or gaze into their presence; then I feel their presence envelop me; and as I relax into that presence, I hear the whispered words, "I love you."

I had a dream the other night with my niece Jennifer in it. Jen is in her early thirties, and she is known for, how do you say nicely—voicing her opinion and being blunt. In my dream, I was meditating, and she said, "Why are you breathing so hard (or loud)?"

When I woke up, I decided the dream meant I should take it easy on myself. That perhaps I'm trying too hard.

day 18

SCORPION COUNT: 1
SNAKE COUNT: 6

Each morning I climb down to my cave carrying a duffel bag and wearing a backpack. The backpack carries four liters of water, journals, and my food for the day. The duffel bag contains two yoga mats, four Bibles, a meditation cushion, and a towel. Today, as I placed my mats, water, Bibles, and meditation pillow under my mosquito net, something bit me squarely in the center of my back while another bug dive-bombed me from the front. So I hurriedly got under the net while being careful not to bang my head on the stone ceiling. I hadn't been lying there for too long before I felt a pinch on my back. It was a red ant—they started biting early today.

Yesterday I saw three snakes, two of which appeared to be mating in the morning sun—the tail halves of their bodies flopping around and sticking out of a hole. The third snake was lying out on the plateau as I went for a walk at 7:30 p.m. It didn't move, so I thought it might be dead. It was a light color—almost white with black slashes across its back. As I looked closer, I saw its tongue flicking out (why do snakes do this?). I walked back to my tent and got my camera. When I returned, the snake was still there, so I snapped a picture.

When boredom sets in like it has today, there are only so many times you can clip your fingernails and toenails, only so many times you can watch the bumblebees or wasps, and only so much of the Gospels you can read before you have to stop.

The desert heat is my prison guard. It decides when I can come out of my cell. Sure, I can attempt a breakout while it's hot, but later on I'll pay for it because I'll be so miserable that years will seemingly be added to my time.

The more you fight the limitations and discomfort or suffering of the desert, the more you suffer.

The desert won't change—*I have to change*.

So as I lay here and complaints from my body come up, I let them be, just as the desert allows whatever rocks emerge from its landscape to be.

If I start thinking of the future and *how nice it will be when I'm out of here*, that comparison of *the future to now* makes the now more unbearable. Besides, I don't want to endure the desert by fantasizing and barring the door to it with hopes of the future. Instead, I want to *live the desert* by opening the door to it.

Occasionally I allow myself a mental excursion into the past or the future (most of the time I can't even stop my mind from doing so), but when I go off to "someplace else," I usually find that upon my return, my body and mind are tense and tight—and have been that way even while I was gone. So this time travel doesn't really get me anywhere, because time passes even more slowly in the desert when the mind and body are tight.

But when I relax and just live in the moment, each breath becomes just like one of the bumblebees that visit my man-made water hole—it comes and it goes.

"Why are you going to the desert?" my brother asked.

Right now I have no answer, nor do I need one.

I've finally broken the code of the black bird with orange on the wings. They talk all the time, and what they say is "R-We-Ree?" Whatever that means.

They also whistle. You know that whistle everybody does? People do it from far away, and it's sort of the "hey you" of whistles. Well, these black birds do it so perfectly that it took me nearly a week before I learned not to turn around every time I heard it.

The coolest thing is the way they ride the wind currents. They have their wings folded at their sides like Olympic down-hill skiers, and they fly so quickly that you hear "whoosh!" as they pass by.

As I sat on a rock down by the edge of the canyon, I almost disappeared. Slowly I let go of that "bundle" of who I think I am—

the Buddhists call it *skandas*. It's a bunch of stuff: thoughts, feelings, bodily sensations that we cling to, grasp in the way that one grasps "pickup sticks." But the Buddhists say, "Hey, all you've got to do is drop the bundle of pickup sticks, and what's left—that's *your true nature*."

So I'm down at the edge—almost forgetting myself—when that image of Moses in the Bible comes up. The one where he asks to see God, but God says, "No man can see Me and live!" (Exodus 33:20 NASB).

Instead, God says he will put his hand over Moses's eyes and pass by; then, once God has passed by, God says, "I will take My hand away and you shall see My back, but My face shall not be seen" (v. 23 NASB).

So when I'm sitting there at the edge, and I begin to let go into the Present, into God's presence, it becomes obvious that you can't watch God's presence appear—you can only surrender into God's presence. But if you come out of that place, only then will you be able to glimpse God's back after he has passed by.

The last thing to die at God's door is that sense of me, of I, of separateness, that desire that wants to see God. It can't pass through the eye of a needle, nor can it look God in the face.

I may have made a mistake. That small, wet hole by the mosquito net—I dug it out so that the insects could drink freely. But today it was constantly swarmed by large bumblebees. The wasp who tried to build a home by me was there, and each time another bumblebee went into the hole, he came out for a second, as though to avoid a confrontation before going back in.

At times, there were four or five or more bees in there with that wasp. His popping out of the hole for a second whenever a new bee showed up must have been some kind of respectful hierarchy sort of thing. He let the bees choose their spots before he sat down.

I meditated for fifty minutes with 20 to 25 mph winds swirling around me. Then at the end I prayed.

"Please, dear Lord—teach me what I need to understand. Teach me in the clearest and straightest way possible—and with as little pain as possible. Please instill your blessing and your love so that I may feel your love even if I suffer."

day 19

Last night I heard a truck approaching at around 10:00 or 11:00 p.m. I thought I heard Arabic songs and chanting. *What if some PLO terrorists are coming to get me?* A week before I got here, some bedouins put two young Israeli men in sacks and stoned them to death. *What if those same bedouins heard I was here and they're coming to get me?*

I jumped out of bed, put on my shorts and sandals, grabbed my cell phone (in case I had to call for help), and went outside to look for the truck—but it was already gone.

I fell asleep last night thinking of food. What could I eat that I haven't eaten for eighteen days in a row? Then I remembered. I have a bag of couscous! My mouth started to water.

"There is no way," I said to my body, "that I'm getting up now to make couscous—you'll just have to wait till tomorrow."

So the following morning at 6:30 a.m., I started cooking couscous in a pot that Tamir had lent me. The pot was dented

and had layers of stuff dried inside—but I didn't care. When
the pot boiled, I tried to cover it with a metal bowl (since Tamir
didn't give me a cover, but the pot tipped over, spilling half of
the couscous onto the ground. I tried to save whatever I could
by attempting to skim off the top of the fallen couscous. But
when the flies and mosquitoes attacked, I hurried so much that
I scraped up more stone and sand than couscous.

I quickly added olive oil and salt to what was left in the pot.
*Should I eat it now with the bugs attacking, or should I go under my
net and relax?* When I had checked earlier that morning, a half
dozen or more bumblebees were already buzzing about my
cave. It was already too hard taking my gear past them without
also having to carry a pot of couscous. I shoveled the couscous
into my mouth and then made my way down the cliff to my
cave. I maneuvered past the bees without incident, but after I
was under the net, periodically one crashed into my net with a
loud *buzzz*. I wasn't sure if it was an aggressive maneuver or just
a navigational miscalculation.

I don't want to meditate or pray.

I want to do anything but go deeper into myself. The spiritual presence I feel is like a bright light that I cannot turn off.
I tried sleeping, but I'm not tired. I lay under my net—but I'm
too aware of myself. I reach for the Bible and read some of
Luke's Gospel. This is the only way I can avoid the *intersection*
of awareness, where God and I meet. But suddenly I'm struck
by the fact that I'm using the Gospels—the story of Jesus—to
avoid God!

That's why I came to the desert. Because *what I knew, thought, or read of God was keeping me from God.*

I finally sat for my morning meditation and prayer. I'm sitting four times a day, at least forty-five minutes each time. On many of the retreats I've been on, we sat one hour at a time, seven to ten times a day. But I've decided not to kill myself here or push myself too hard in this regard. As it is, I'm practically in a constant state of meditation or prayer—there is nowhere to run from myself and nowhere to run from God. Relating to God is often done through a verbalized prayer, and whether I'm saying "I love you" or "I hate you" or "Help me" or "Leave me alone," they're all prayers, all ways of relating to God.

In my morning meditation, I'm very aware of how angry I am at being here. I don't like the pain in my legs or back, nor do I like the pain of my soul as I go deeper. Why do I do this? Do I have to do this? For some reason, I stumble along and keep going.

Since the bees have been swarming the last few days, I haven't seen my gecko friends.

When your three-day-old baby soils her diaper, do you have to forgive her? No—you love her. It is the same with God—we are like three-day-old sons and daughters to him. When we soil ourselves, there is no need for forgiveness—he only loves us.

We use words and concepts to speak and talk about Jesus and God. But who they really are is beyond concept or word. The trick is to *use* concepts and words and not get caught in them.

As I meditate, I hear the bumblebees crowd around the small water hole. They buzz together in such a deep and energetic way that they sound like a bunch of Tibetan lamas huddled together and chanting.

As the bees fly from the water hole, they all make the same sound or tone—it's the "Om" of Hinduism. So now I'm constantly hearing the sound that for more than a billion Hindus is the sound of God bringing all things into existence.

day 20

It's day 20! Halfway home!

I don't think of going home very often, but when I do it's enjoyable. But after my fantasizing is done, it's worse for a while because, somehow, bringing the future into the here and now sets up a subtle or not-so-subtle resistance to the here and now. So which is more pleasurable—this "now" of desert with all its heat and bugs and not one flat spot to sleep or sit on, or the "future" of being at home in the States with all the food I want, a shower, a comfortable chair, a bed, and great friends?

The future of "being at home" is easily the most desirable. But when I cling to thoughts of that future, my soul contracts so tightly that this "tense holding" actually becomes the center of my universe. Life in the desert is then seen from and through this distorted contraction. Then my whole stay here becomes even more filled with suffering because I'm living through my view of the desert and not the desert as it is. My stay in the desert then opposes the desert and lives alongside the desert— instead of being part of the desert. And isn't that what Jesus meant in the Garden of Gethsemane when he said, "Not my

will, but thine, be done" (Luke 22:42 KJV)? That any ego contraction made within the Spirit leads to the perception and
experience of separation from Spirit?

I've often lived like that! Not able to relax, to be free—to live
the "life in full" (see John 10:10), as Jesus called it. Instead, I
cling stubbornly to parts of life and parts of myself—which
only separates me from the freedom that comes from relaxing
into a full acceptance of Spirit.

When I look at the faces of people I meet, sometimes I see
the faces of souls who are holding tight to something. I see the
lines of endurance and will on their faces and the tightness of
mind in their bodies. That way of life is fine when you don't
know any better (and it may even be appropriate at times). But
when you've had a born-again or religious experience in which
you become the freedom of spirit that we were born to be, then
that grasping, tight, and willful way of life no longer feeds you.
Sure, you can survive using those abilities, but to keep living
that way after it's served its purpose is to know what Jesus
meant by "the spiritually dead" (Luke 9:59 NLT).

"Bill, why are you going to the desert?" my brother asked.

Though I didn't have time to give him an answer, I think he's
beginning to understand. He himself is getting older, and our
oldest brother died a few years ago. To realize one's own mortality through the death of a loved one is one way of going to
the desert without actually going there.

So what is the desert?

The desert is a state of being—a place where you find
yourself alone, even in the midst of many. In this place, a
place that has now begun to occupy your regular world, you
encounter a disease (a dis-ease): a dryness, a barrenness, and

an aloneness—alone because no one can bloom the desert for you. Not your wife, or your job, or your friends—not even your children can save you from the desert, even as they come running to you one moment and move away from you as adults in the next.

No one can help you with the question the desert poses—and no one can help you realize the answer. Your friends and teachers can tell you what to take with you to the desert (such as compassion, grief, focus, and prayer), what to watch out for in the desert (such as poisonous emotions, biting thoughts, fear-laden cliffs and edges), and to beware of the most terrifying of all desert creatures—the unknown. But no one can save you from all the monsters and demons you will meet in the desert, because those monsters and demons are you—and have always been you—parts of yourself kept away by a busyness that was useful only outside the desert.

Of all human capacities, the ability to be still is most valuable in the desert. It keeps you alive in a harsh environment where one wrong move can tumble you over a cliff; where a too-quickly made step can find you walking up the back of a poisonous snake; and where an impetuous reach of your hand can be met with the wrath of a scorpion's sting. So stillness and then action, not rash action or reaction, are called for. But herein lies the problem. By being still—perhaps still for the first time in your life—all monsters, demons, and dark avoidances know where to find you. They will come to you at the most frightening and inopportune time—at night. And the desert, like all places on earth, most definitely has a night—a very dark night.

And if one brings the busyness of the day into the dark night

of the desert in order to ward off the darkness, that busyness
will only make the dark night even darker.

I hiked up to the hostel, which is about two to three miles away.
I must be acclimated to the desert, because I left at 9:30 a.m.,
a time of the day I would have thought too hot, and yet I am
invigorated. I needed to drop off my three 50-liter water bottles to be refilled. Tamir is out of town on a wilderness trek with
his class in Jerusalem, so Ya'el, who lives at the hostel, is bringing my weekly supply of water tomorrow. Actually, I hope she
brings four bottles. An extra bottle allows me to wipe myself
down every night with a cloth so that I don't stick to my bed or
sleeping bag at night.

The walk gave me a feeling of space, because in my meditation and most of the day I am trapped in this mosquito net.
After twenty days in the desert, I also trusted my knowledge of
the surroundings enough to take a shortcut over several hills.
When I first got to the desert, it all looked the same: brown and
tan cliffs, plateaus, and rolling hills. But now I have a few landmarks by which I navigate. Besides the Dead Sea and the
memorial on the hill, there is a hill with rocks piled on top and
an aerial from an Israeli army post near the hostel, the top of
which is visible.

Also, when I first got to the desert, walking up and down
a hill was difficult because there were so many rocks and
sudden drop-offs to contend with. But as I relax into the
desert, I am able to look at a hillside or a cliff before I climb
up and see the path of least resistance—I see the best way up

and down. Just as in life, if you are "still" and open, the way will reveal itself.

My plan was to drop off the bottles at the hostel and leave without talking to anyone. No one saw me arrive because I came from the desert side and found a way through the barbed wire. I felt a bit like Lawrence of Arabia when he and fifty bedouins surprised the Turkish army by crossing the Nefud Desert and attacking from a direction thought impossible.

"I'll leave a key for you behind the flowerpot," Ya'el had said. "In case you come and need something when I'm not here."

I let myself into Ya'el's apartment and left a list of supplies I needed. I was sick of nuts and dried fruit—and especially sick of the white rice pasta. I don't know what it was about the desert, but my body started to crave real food (although less of it)—and the white rice pasta tasted like nothing but a bunch of bleached and nutrient-less glop going down.

I looked in Ya'el's cupboard and—jackpot! Tuna! I had been thinking about tuna for the last few days. You can't be alone out in the desert, praying and meditating and reading in the Gospels about a bunch of fishermen and how many fish they catch every time Jesus is around or how Jesus multiplies the loaves and fish to feed thousands or how the resurrected Jesus is fed broiled fish by the apostles without thinking, *Yes—fish would be good about now!*

I grabbed two cans of tuna along with a couple of apples and turned to leave. But before I did, I stopped and took in what had actually been the first thing I had noticed—couldn't help but notice when I opened the door to her apartment—which was that Ya'el's place smelled like a woman: exotic and sensual. And it was so colorful. Pink and green candles on the tables.

Various healing stones and crystals placed just so—creating little altars throughout her living space. There were pictures and statues of dolphins everywhere—even books about dolphins. One dolphin book was about dolphin therapy and how being with dolphins helps people. The authors even did a study that showed how human brain activity changed before and after playing with dolphins.

It was all so vivid—small explosions of color and smell. It was as though I had been living in a world devoid of color for weeks, and now it was all so beautiful. That's why I went to the desert, so that I'd love and appreciate life more. If you are happy with nothing, then everything else becomes a wonder—an added joy.

As I walked back to my cave, I bit into an apple. *Wow! This is really something—it crunches and is alive.* I looked at the bite I took out of the apple, and the apple glistened in the sun. It sparkled, and it radiated a light—a very clear, luminous aliveness. *Wow!* I thought again. *This is amazing.*

That's why I went to the desert, so that an apple would be amazing.

I lost my mala, or rosary (which Mother Teresa and the Dalai Lama had blessed) while walking through the desert to the hostel. I put the sandalwood rosary (which I had been praying with) on the ground when I stopped to better tie the three 50-liter bottles to my backpack. It's just about the color of the sand and stone it was lying on. But I have a few others, so if you ever find a sandalwood mala rosary in the middle of the Judean desert—it's yours.

Being in the Judean desert demands a steep learning curve. Especially for someone like me who never really camped. I took out my Swiss Army knife and found what looked like a can opener. I placed the blade on top of the tuna can with the hooked bottom edge wedged against the edge of the can. With a slightly torqued upward motion, I made a two-inch opening in the can. I tried to make another cut and somehow sliced the side of the can. Oil ran out all over the foam pad under my mosquito net.

"That was smart!" I said out loud to the only idiot present.

Eventually, after spilling the oil a few more times and making a complete mess (which I hoped wouldn't draw hordes of red ants), I dumped the excess oil over a cliff. Then I tasted the tuna—magnificent!

As I ate it, I kept thinking of Jesus eating that broiled fish. And then I started singing, "What's the best tuna you'll happen to see? Ask any tuna—Chicken of the Sea."

It was a really catchy tune, and my foot was moving up and down as I sang it over and over again. Then I looked at the label. It wasn't Chicken of the Sea—it was Starkist. And the big fish on the side wore black sunglasses and a red hat or fin on his head.

"I remember that guy," I said. "That's Charlie Tuna."

But even as I studied Charlie Tuna's familiar face, I found myself singing, "Ask any tuna you happen to see . . ."

And it became clear to me why the "Chicken of the Sea" ad campaign was vastly superior to that of Charlie Tuna.

On the inside cover of my journal are a few notes I have written:

Love is an understanding that happens *now*, not yesterday.
Love doesn't grow—we, the experiencers of love, grow.

For now, I'll let the bumblebees stay. I actually like their company very much. Their sounds resonate with me and, as I said, remind me of chanting Tibetan monks. When I have to pass them to climb out of (or into) my cave, I come within inches of where they are collecting. I try to avoid any movements they may misinterpret as aggressive. I also try avoiding an accidental collision with one. Occasionally I'll be passing the water hole at the same moment that one of them is coming or going. I will freeze, and sometimes the bee does too. We look like two people who, while trying to pass each other in the hallway, keep mirroring the other's attempts at getting by. Finally, I will totally stop, then slowly step to the side while the bumblebee goes by.

They must be worker bees for the hive—water bearers. It took them two weeks to discover this water pit, the size of a small cantaloupe at its opening; then they funneled down to what amounts to an area of wet sand the size of a silver dollar. I can hear them nuzzling down into that wet sand, pulling from it the water their hive needs for life.

That's why Jesus went into the desert. To go deeper and

farther into the depths and pull from it the sustenance both he and all people need for life.

Up on the plateau, I saw a beautiful black-and-white bird. It sat on a rock not more than fifteen feet from me (which is unusual).

"You're a beautiful bird!" I said.

Suddenly I realized why he's sitting there. He's waiting for something. Sure enough, something crawls out from under a rock, and he attacks again and again but can't quite pick it up. It crawled under another rock, and when I went to see what it was, the bird flew away.

Underneath the rock was a wounded bumblebee that buzzed as I uncovered it. It half flew, half crawled over to another rock. I left it alone, to its own fate.

I hear a noise as I lay under my mosquito net. I look to my right and see that it's a fat brown mouse with a gray, beardy face. It looks like the same mouse I caught snooping around my gear after my walk this morning.

"Great. That's all I need. Mice chomping at my food and chewing holes in my backpacks to get at the food."

But the mice are so cute and friendly looking that they're hard to resist. I mean, Sandy my gecko friend is not exactly "warm." Actually, he's probably a cold-blooded reptile—so he has an excuse.

The other day I did toss a date and a nut (stuck together)

over where I had seen a mouse. But he never came out from under the rock face to get it. I think of feeding the mice, but that would only bring them closer to where I live, sleep, and eat. That is probably a recipe for disaster.

For a moment I bask in the picture of mice eating out of my hand as if I were some kind of Saint Francis or something. Then I imagine people watching me as though I were Saint Francis. Finally, I drop the whole fantasy and lay back down.

One other disappointment to report: On the way back from the hostel, I saw a guy standing next to a tent on the other side of a ridge about a quarter to a half mile from me.

"Dude!" I wanted to yell. "Go away!"

He had pitched his tent on top of a plateau. That's a nice idea, but the night winds—which come between 4:00 p.m. and 6:00 p.m.—will blow over his tent. Also, I don't know where he's going to stay during the heat of the day. Unless there's a cave over there—but I doubt it. For sure he isn't bunking in my cave.

day 21

(DREAM 1)

I dreamed that I was walking with three people. I suddenly realized I was dreaming just as one of the other three said, "Are we dreaming?"

I said, "Yes—I think so."

The third person said they thought they were dreaming too.

"I've never been in a dream before where this many people knew it was a dream," I said, excited.

(DREAM 2)

I walked into a nightclub/bar. I knew I was dreaming.

"Are you from the airline?" the female bartender asked.

"No," I said, and then I thought I heard someone at a table talking about being awake in the "dreaming."

"Is everyone in this place aware that they're sleeping and dreaming?"

"No," the bartender said. "About one-third of these people are actually buried over in the graveyard."

Our relationship with God is like a man who is at home in his bed asleep. He dreams that he is far away from home, and he is tired—and he wishes he were at home in his bed asleep.

For some reason, I keep having the strange feeling and thought that I won't get out of the desert alive; that I won't live to see my forty days completed; that I will die before I have a chance to go back home and see Bonnie and my friends—and look back on this accomplishment. It's as though it's too much of an accomplishment for me, and I wouldn't be allowed by the Spirit to look back on it and reflect; that somehow that would make me too happy—and maybe I don't believe I can be that happy and be allowed to live.

The Bible says we are made in the image of God. If we become what we were made to be, we fall into the face of God.

My meditation all seems to be about pleasure. Feeling the pleasure that is a natural part of the heart. I detect a lot of fear, a reticence to become sensitive enough to accept and feel that pleasure because I crave it so much. Am I afraid the source of that pleasure will control me or even take it away from me?

As I let myself experience the pleasure that's always present, I soften, and then I come upon even deeper layers of fear. A fear of pleasure or perhaps joy?

I was awakened from my nap with the feeling that someone or something had just hit me solidly on the top of my head. My skull was still vibrating from the blow as I opened my eyes.

While lying on my side, I saw a black-and-white bird chase two plump, furry mice out from under a rocky ledge. The mice scattered in opposite directions as the bird hopped up and down a few times as if to say, ". . . and don't come back!"

I just pigged out! I drank an iced coffee! Ya'el just brought my weekly supply of water, and she brought some ice as a treat. She also brought four cans of tuna, a high-fiber cereal, and whole-wheat pitas. I mixed up some instant coffee with some dry nondairy creamer and sugar. Normally, back in the States, I wouldn't have touched such a foul concoction, but here in the Judean desert—the land of milk and honey—it's an absolute treat and a godsend.

Sometimes in meditation when I see the hidden agony of my soul, it's overwhelming and I'm ready to give up. The irony is that after I give up or surrender, the spring comes; the morning comes, and God's light releases within and all around me. Then of course, during those times when I'm so exhausted from the heat, prayer, and meditation, an iced coffee isn't too bad either.

I'm astonished by the extent of the agony I find in my soul. Usually this agony is hidden, and only its reflection is seen; it's in the way people cannot be present with you. It's in the shifting, vacant, or overly intense eyes. It's in the anxious or rigid body posture. It's the lack of spirit in people's words and touch. God has been kind to us by making us blind to what is within, because if God were to open up the true state of our souls to ourselves, we would be devastated, destroyed, overwhelmed by the pain and horror. What pain and horror? There's a secret that's actually not so secret—and it goes something like this: we are more connected to one another than we could ever imagine, and the truth of everything we see, say, or touch makes an imprint on our soul. "The truth of everything" is very important to understand because it means that even if we ignore something, the truth of it still imprints on us. If we ignore all the hurts done to ourselves and others, the truth still collects. It collects in the soul, and if you ever look into that place, you will see a myriad of tears, yours and theirs.

That's why I went to the desert, so that I could see the tears I've collected through eons of ignoring the true state of my soul.

I came to the desert to witness.

I came to the desert to be what I am.

I came to the desert to cry.

In our lives, we've had many conversations, but hardly anyone has talked with us. In our lives, so many people have looked at us, but only few have seen us. Two thousand years ago there was a man who talked to us, and still our ears and hearts burn. Two thousand years ago there was a man who saw us, and our eyes are still recovering from having looked into the sun.

Two thousand years ago there was a man who said he was a human being, and still we don't believe him.

I hear Jesus saying, "I am the Son of Man," which means "I am a human being."

I hear Jesus saying, "We are all sons and daughters of God," when he says, "I am returning to my Father and your Father" (John 20:17).

I hear Jesus exalting what human beings are destined to be when he says, "Now is the Son of Man glorified and God is glorified in him" (John 13:31).

I hear Jesus saying, "You are in me, and I am in you" (John 14:20), even as he was dying on the cross, so that in truth we were all crucified that day in ways we haven't even realized yet.

And finally I hear Jesus saying, "I and the Father are one" (John 10:30 NASB), and since we are in Jesus and he in us, we are also One with the Father. This, above all things, was his message to us. That we would be One with the Father as was he—that we would realize we were One with the Father as he did. The prodigal son—no matter how far he has strayed from his father—is always his father's son.

Jesus said, "The Son of Man has authority on earth to forgive sins" (Matthew 9:6), and each of us, as a son of man and a human being, has the capacity to forgive sins. Actually, what human beings are really doing is not forgiving sins, but commenting on what is already true in the depth of the Supreme Being—that our sins are already forgiven.

day 22

I waited until 9:00 p.m. when all the bees were gone. Then I kicked sand into the water hole till it no longer existed. What had begun as a place for a few insects to gather had become monopolized by the bees, and just like the Borg on *Star Trek*, the water hole had been assimilated by the bees until it was theirs *only*.

When there had been only one or two bees, or even five or six, that was okay with me. But then it got to be where there were ten to twelve bees constantly at the water hole and others constantly coming and going. They began to attack my mosquito net. First one—then up to three at a time. I often took a longer route to the cave to avoid them. And there were a couple of "directionally challenged" bees who were always getting caught every ten minutes behind my net. I tried to help direct them out, but they must have been male bees, because they wouldn't take my directions, and they even attacked me.

So I filled the water hole in and then went about sixty yards away to a place where Tamir said there might be water if I dug. I figured if I dug them another water hole, I wouldn't feel guilty. I dug with my spoon, but I didn't see any water. A few bees were hovering over me, watching. I didn't like the guilt trip they were putting on me. I turned and looked at them.

"There's a bunch of water over there," I said, pointing toward the Dead Sea less than a mile away. I knew the water at the Dead Sea was too salty for the bees, but there were fresh pools of water there also, water that was called "sweet water," which the bees could easily use.

"I'd go there if I could," I said, referring to the thousand-foot cliff that separated me from the Dead Sea, "but you guys could fly there easily."

The bees continued to hover overhead—waiting for water.

"Just . . . go over . . . there!" I said, pointing to the Dead Sea again. But the bees wouldn't budge.

"I'm not going to feel guilty about this," I told them as I walked away. "There's just no way."

"Did you take a shower at my house?" Ya'el asked when she dropped off my weekly water supply.

"No," I said, "it felt as though I would be cheating."

Ya'el rolled her eyes, saying, "You and Tamir have this thing . . . ," but she didn't finish; instead, she just dismissed me with a wave of her hand.

In my meditation, I'm finding that I'm angry and I don't even know why. I'm so angry I want to pound the floor or punch the ceiling of the cave. But that would only hurt me. To make it worse, by mistake I dribbled a small amount of water next to my net—a tablespoon perhaps—and the bees are going crazy. They're constantly flying into my net and buzzing as they look for its source. The sound gets very loud, and they keep it up twenty, thirty, thirty-five minutes into my meditation.

"Shut up!" I yell at the top of my lungs. But of course they act as though they didn't hear me. I laugh at myself, partly because I'm yelling at insects as though they're going to listen, and partly because it feels good to yell: a good, clean, unrestricted desert yell.

I return to meditation and prayer—still so angry that I don't know what to do. Should I squeeze a towel and say my resentments like in therapy, or just keep meditating? Part of me is fighting my anger, squeezing the anger down till that angry part of me is knotted up and almost dead. Just as I'm ready to quit meditating, I tell myself no because I vowed to meditate till 10:00 a.m.—and that's fifty-two more minutes.

I keep meditating, and the cycle of tensing, relaxing, tensing, relaxing continues, with the anger coming in waves. When 10:00 a.m. finally comes, I lie down. I'm surrounded by buzzing bees, and I fantasize about smashing every one of them into bits in order to silence them. If I could only allow myself to be angry—to be angry totally—then maybe it would all come out and end?

I want coffee again today. But I have to limit myself. The caffeine speeds up my thoughts and tenses my body, which is not conducive to going deeper. I've limited myself to a half cup every three days.

I had a dream that I was walking around Madison and watching a TV show on a big screen that was over a Madison bank. At the same time, the actors were performing the parts in front of the bank. I don't understand how they could be shooting the episode now, when I'm watching it on the big screen. Then I realize I don't have the job I thought I did (a job that gives me time to wander around); instead, I'm supposed to be at that job now. I've screwed up!

Later a woman tells me they really want me to work there, so I figure I've got another chance, but I make the same mistake again! Then I'm running down the street with a ski mask on. I guess I'm out of control, because I trip and do a head-over-heels fall; then I tumble, rolling over once, and I'm right back up running again, without skipping a beat. I hear someone laugh. Obviously they saw my mistake. But I'm partly comforted by the fact I have a mask on and people probably couldn't recognize me.

What does the dream mean? That I'm doing the retreat wrong? Because everything in the dream says I'm confused and wrong. Actually, I've been thinking that I'm doing it wrong. So let's just play along. What would be the right way?

If I was praying twenty-four hours a day and in constant bliss and communion with God, that would be the right way! Pretty heavy demands on myself, I'd say. But then God says, "You did the right thing by coming here for forty days. There is nothing else you have to do. Whatever happens in these forty days is for your healing."

Then a deep sadness wells up from within me as I realize

there has always been a secret, hidden part of me that has always felt I'm not doing things right or good enough. Jesus had his temptations, the Buddha had his, and I have mine. When a human being sees the error of his ways, the temptation is to judge, sentence, and inflict punishment. But this is the way of Adam and Eve and all their offspring, and it never solved the problem.

The real problem was not that Adam and Eve sinned or got it wrong. Their real problem was that they hid themselves from a loving God. They hid their fear and hid their shame and most of all hid their pain at being separated from the love they felt with God.

I came to the desert—not to judge—but to love. Not to condemn or push away my children of fear, shame, and loss—but to pull my children close. To hold them close, to be with them until my house is no longer divided against itself. Jesus said, "Permit the children to come to Me; do not hinder them; for the kingdom of God belongs to such as these" (Mark 10:14 NASB).

It was quiet, so quiet for the first time in days. The bees had gone and taken their buzzing with them. Toward the end of my meditation, I heard a racket to my right. I opened my eyes and saw a pudgy mouse chasing a three-foot snake less than two feet in front of me. The mouse almost caught him till the snake slithered and then slid down a thirty-foot rock face like a reptilian toboggan. The mouse skidded to a stop and then turned around—walking proudly back.

"I'm impressed," I said. "That was very impressive."

The mouse perked up his ears and then sniffed with his nose. Then he turned and looked right at me. His eyes got as big as saucers, and he ran back under a rock ledge.

Yesterday the bird chased the mouse. Today the mouse chased the snake. I wonder who will chase whom tomorrow?

As I go through my forty days, I find that I am just sitting, just eating, just sleeping. The desert does that to you.

"It's too hot!" I could complain to myself out here in the desert. "It's just too hot!"

But what's the point? I can't go into an air-conditioned room.

"So it's too hot for you?" I ask myself.

"Yes—it's too hot!" I reply.

"So what," I say.

"This food is boring!" I say.

"The food's boring?"

"Yeah!"

"So what?"

"The rocks hurt my rear end!"

"The rocks hurt your rear end?"

"Yeah!"

"So what?"

It's then I realize standing outside "it" and complaining about "it" does no good; in fact, it makes "it" worse. So I bring my focus from what it isn't to what it is. And I just do it. I am it. And time passes.

day 23

I went to bed last night wishing Jesus would pay me a visit, though not in the spiritual sense, because I already experience that from time to time. I want to see him in a body. It would be nice if he just came by and knocked on my tent.

"Hello?" he'd say. "Anyone home?"

Even a dream with him would be okay. Sometimes a dream is very real, and we could have a nice conversation, and I'd remember most of it. I had a dream years ago with Jesus in it. This dream was a "lucid" dream, in that after it began, I knew I was dreaming. Since I was dreaming and I have some power over my dreams, I focused on meeting Jesus. Then I found him working in a butcher shop—you know, cutting up sides of beef, grinding hamburger, and selling chops. When I asked if I could talk to him, he said, "Meet me at the yoga studio at 4:00 p.m." During the dream, I had to keep focusing my awareness in a balanced way so that I wouldn't "lose the dream"—either by falling back asleep inside the dream or by becoming too strongly aware, thus causing the dream to break up and myself to awaken.

Anyway, I'm going along in my dream—*focused*. I got out of

a taxi at 4:00 p.m. in front of the yoga studio in order to meet Jesus. As I reached into my pocket to get some small change for the cabdriver, my focus changed from keeping the dream going to frustration. There were some coins at the bottom of my pocket that I couldn't quite get at, and my efforts turned into frustration. That frustration broke my focus and the dream fell apart. I woke up.

I decided the dream meant that "details" I considered "small change" were actually very important and could block my plans if I didn't deal with them correctly.

Also, it told me that my frustration with "small change" or "details" was a problem.

My meditation is often difficult. Then it changes in a moment to bliss—timelessness.

At the end of meditation today, I was very aware of Jesus's presence. I decided to meditate on him, with him, letting go into him. I was in the midst of love.

"This love," I asked Jesus, "is this you?"

"It's us," he said. "It's what we are."

"But sometimes it seems like you," I said.

"Reflections in a pool," he said. "Reflections in a pool."

"No, thank you," I said. "I'll just watch you do it."

"Are you sure?" the man named Eli asked.

"I'm sure," I said. "I'll just watch you do it."

Fifteen minutes earlier I'd heard a car drive up on the plateau. I could tell it was very close to my tent. I climbed out of my cave to make sure my tent wasn't being robbed. Six men piled out of a four-wheel drive. They looked like tourists. I suddenly felt slightly territorial.

"Shalom," said the first man—a stocky, dark-skinned man with tattooed arms, designer sunglasses, and a cocky way about him. I felt an immediate dislike for him—because I usually don't like such obvious strutting.

"Hello," I said.

Each of them took turns introducing themselves and saying, "Shalom"—which is Hebrew for "peace."

"Have you seen hooks around here—for climbing?" he asked.

"Yeah," I said, "down by the edge there are a few hooks."

"We are climbing down," he said. "I am an instructor."

We talked a little longer, and then he asked, "Why are you here?"

"I've been here for four weeks—and I'm staying forty days."

"Really?" he asked.

"Yeah."

"Why?"

I didn't want to give them the "I wrote a Jesus book" spiel right away, because if they were Jewish, Jesus was kind of a bad way to start off a conversation. The Jewish people have been persecuted and blamed for Jesus's death because of the Gospels— the Gospel of John, to be exact. Though John is perhaps the most beautiful and profound of the Gospels, it is also the most anti-Semitic. Why? Because in the first three Gospels, the people who call for Jesus's crucifixion are referred to as "they" or "the crowd," but in John they are called "the Jews." I once counted occurrences of the term "the Jews" in the Gospels and found that it is used eighty times: six times in Matthew, five times in Mark, five times in Luke, and *sixty-four times in John*. Now why is John like this? Especially when all the apostles, the Gospel writers—except for Luke, who may have been Greek—and Jesus were Jewish?

Any scholar will tell you—and this is the great value of recent scholarship—that the Gospel of John was the last Gospel written. It was written after the synagogues had expelled Jewish Christians from their houses of worship. Why? Because, first of all, being a Jew meant you obeyed certain dietary laws and were circumcised. But Paul told new non-Jewish converts that they didn't have to be circumcised or follow dietary laws to follow Jesus. The synagogues said, "Well, you're not really Jews, then—take a hike!"

After being expelled, the tensions between religious factions really set in, and the Gospel of John was written at the time when the Jesus followers, or "the Way" as they were called, were competing against Judaism for new converts, with each side claiming they had the best prophets and teachings.

So I've seen that hurt look in many Jews' eyes when I've mentioned Jesus. Later I confided in Savyon, who was one of the climbers/rappellers, that Jesus would have been heartbroken to see what has been done to his people in his name. As I said that, I almost started to cry.

So when I first met the group of Israelis, I didn't want to focus too much on Jesus.

"I'm staying here for spiritual and religious reasons," I told them. "Jesus was in the desert forty days, Moses was on the mountain for forty days (with God), and it took Elijah forty days and nights of travel to reach Horeb—the mountain of God. Forty days is an important number."

"There's a famous rabbi who stayed in the desert fifteen years," Eli said. "That was a few hundred years ago."

"No way I'm staying here fifteen years," I said. "Forty days, and I'm history."

I showed them my cave, and that's when Eli asked, "You want to climb down with us?"

I almost laughed in his face, because if he would have known the fear I have of heights and how that "edge" they were about to climb over and down had been an integral part of my stay here so far, he would have laughed himself.

"No—I'll watch you do it," I said.

"You sure?"

"I'm sure," I said, never surer of anything in my life. But as I walked with them to the edge, I began thinking about climbing down with them.

Don't be ridiculous, I told myself. *You are afraid of heights. They make you dizzy—and you have that weird compulsion to jump— forget about it!*

I forgot about it—for a moment.

It's foolish to even consider it, I said to myself. *And besides, I was here for forty days to pray and meditate—not to climb down a thousand-foot cliff. Besides, I would be talking with them too much, and it would wreck part of why I'm here—to be silent. It would also wreck the meditative concentration I have built up over these past four weeks.*

No way, I told myself. *I'm not going—besides, I'm scared.*

While I watched them unpack their gear at the edge, Eli asked again if I wanted to climb down with them.

"No," I said. "Not me."

"You sure?" he asked with a bravado that at once challenged me while also telling me that what he was asking me to do was "no big deal." It made me distrust him—his need to do dangerous things combined with his need to be nonchalant about them. I thought, *This is the kind of guy who tries dangerous things before he is ready*. There was no way I was going to trust him with my life, so I started talking to his brother, Ohad.

"Oh yes, I was very afraid of heights when I started," Ohad said. "That's why I did it. I started with five meters, then ten, then fifteen, and after fifteen meters it doesn't matter how far you rappel. I used to be so afraid to look over the edge—I still am."

Then he said it, the words that actually made me trust him.

"I was so afraid I felt like I wanted to jump," he said.

"You did?" I asked, feeling camaraderie with someone who felt how I felt. "Why, do you think?" I asked.

"I think . . . ," he said, pausing—his eyes looking downward as he went solemnly inside himself.

"I think because it is so beautiful," he said, looking up at me with a smile so bright it rivaled the sunrise. "It's so beautiful that I just want to jump into it. It's so beautiful that I just want to go toward it."

I looked around at the Israeli men who were climbing down. There was Eli, who looked Palestinian; his brother, Ohad, who looked Spanish; their father, Mayer, who looked Italian; and a clear-blue-eyed man with a hook nose—he looked Turkish. His brother Savyon, who seemed innocent and gentle—looked French. And Coby, who was thin and always smiling (and smoking)—looked as though he worked on fishing boats off the Florida coast.

A war started to be waged in my soul. Should I try it? Maybe God wants me to try it. It's too much of a coincidence that *I'm afraid of the edge, and these guys show up who want to take me over the edge.*

Bill, stop it, I said to myself. *You're playing games with yourself. It's ridiculous for you to consider it. It's foolish. You're letting some macho-challenge thing convince you to do something way out of your league. You have to practice this sort of thing in safety first. What if you died biting off more than you can handle? Or you froze on the way down and they had to come rescue you?*

So I asked Jesus what he thought.

"We love you, Bill," was all he would say. He wouldn't commit himself one way or the other—or give me a hint of what to do.

"Bill?" Eli asked again. "You sure you don't want to go down?"

"Can I do it?" I asked. "I've never done this kind of thing before."

"You can do it," he assured me. "*Any man* can do it."

Well, I was a man, but I wasn't sure I was *that* much of a man. I looked over at Ohad. I trusted him.

"You think I can do it?"

"Yes," he said, "you can do it."

I ran back to my tent and put on a shirt along with Dave's climbing boots. How often did Dave wear these boots? They looked almost new. And when did he wear them? Did he ever wear them to descend? To go over the edge?

I couldn't believe I was doing this. As I walked down toward the Israelis waiting at the edge, I stepped on a rock and it gave way. I instinctively put down my hand and righted myself. Was that an omen warning me that I shouldn't go? Or was it an omen showing me that I can recover from a misstep or mistake?

I went over to the edge and sat down. Actually, I was three feet from the edge, and I refused to look in its direction.

Oh, God, how am I going to climb over the edge, I thought, *when I can't even look over the edge?*

I watched several guys go down. I tried to get some sense of what I was going to do. I also tried to look relaxed, as though I were playing golf and waiting for my turn to tee off. It was hot, and I climbed under the shade of an overhanging rock.

"Bill, you want a drink of water?" Eli asked.

"Yeah."

He handed me the bottle, and I took a few swigs—then I felt nauseated.

Oh no, I'm going to puke!

I stopped drinking the water, hoping that would stave off any vomiting midway through my descent. Then my stomach started to grumble and to rumble. I was so scared that I suddenly felt I was going to have diarrhea.

I squeezed my buttocks and tightened my jaw. Just then Eli looked at me. I tried to look calm even as I was squeezing my butt cheeks together.

"Okay, Bill, you're up," Eli said.

This was it. Was I supposed to be a man and go over the

edge? Or was I supposed to be even braver and say, "Eli, I've decided not to"?

"Here's your harness," he said.

I began to put it on, hoping I wouldn't trip as I put my right and then left leg through. Eli grabbed the buckle and cinched it up tight for me.

"Feel all right?" he asked.

"Yeah."

"Tuck in your shirt," he said, "and pull down your pant legs more. That will protect your skin. You will have two ropes with you: one I will control, called belaying; the other you control. You can't fall, because I'm controlling one rope, okay? This is much safer. Most important, keep your legs shoulder width apart—no more. If they are too wide, you will sit down on the side of the cliff face. If they are too close together, you will do like a barn door and swing side to side. And if we yell, don't look up—look down, because a rock is coming. This rope, hold at your side—by your hip. It is like a brake; pull it down to stop, and let go a little when you want to take steps down."

I suddenly saw myself panicking midway down.

"What if I pulled up during my panic and not down?" I asked.

Eli assured me he had control of his rope *no matter what*. I started over the edge—walking backward.

"Keep your back straight," he said.

Before I knew it, I was sitting on my butt, only twenty feet down the side of the cliff and 250 feet from the ground below. I was doing what rappellers call "the turtle."

"Get your legs under you," he said, "and pull down on the rope."

I followed his directions and somehow found myself standing up again—perpendicular to the side of the cliff. I started walking backward again. My breathing was very heavy. I could tell I was using my breath to pace and focus myself. A couple of times, while walking backward down the cliff, I stepped off an overhang.

"Bill," Eli yelled, "just relax and slide down—use your left hand to help steady you against the cliff as you free-rappel."

I did everything he said, and then my right hand started to burn as the rope ran through it. I tried to stop, but my hand was too high up on the rope.

"Your finger could have got caught in the ring on your harness," Eli later told me, "and it would have broken or been torn off."

"Are you okay?" they yelled, because I had managed to stop twenty meters from the bottom.

"Yeah, I'm okay," I yelled back. "My hand hurts."

"Let go of the rope," someone yelled, "and Eli will feed your rope the rest of the way."

I did as they said and walked backward down the face of the cliff. Then it happened; I hit bottom. Coby was already smoking a cigarette and making Turkish coffee for everyone. I had a small cup and was happy about my accomplishment.

"So we're done?" I asked.

"No," said Zac, a monk-looking man with close-cropped hair and clear blue eyes, "we have another cliff."

"What?" I said. "I thought we were done . . ."

Zac didn't answer; instead, he was busy arranging gear for the next descent. I suddenly deflated, because I thought I was done. *I want to be done!* I had climbed down despite my fear; wasn't that enough? *Why can't I be done?*

I looked up at the cliff I had just climbed down and knew there was no way I could climb back up to my cave. Then I looked at the cliffs all around me; there was no way out—except to climb down the next cliff.

Ohad, who was studying to be a medic, offered to tape up my finger. Half the skin on my knuckle had been burned off, and my hand was all black from rope burns.

Just then I heard a crash—the sound of someone falling and crying out in pain. It was Eli—he had fallen onto a ledge about five meters from the top of the cliff. His father and brother yelled to him, but Eli was too hurt and groggy to reply. He wobbled to and fro as he held on to the rope and fought to maintain consciousness. I was worried he'd pass out and fall the final two hundred feet. Ohad, an excellent rock climber, thought about climbing back up, but Eli managed to clear his head and lower himself down. He had banged up his arm, hit his head, and burned his hand so badly that he had instant blister burns. I tried to focus on Eli's welfare, but all I could think was, *This is the guy who assured me that I was safe, and he just almost killed himself?*

I went over the edge again. Halfway down, my hand was burning, but I hung on until I finished. It was a sixty-meter descent.

"We have another cliff," someone said.

"We aren't done?" I asked again. "I thought we were done."

Eli walked by, and with a big, understanding grin, he said, "Bill—*enjoy the day!*"

No Zen master could have said it better. I immediately let go of my wants—just like in my meditation—and opened to the moment. I even smiled a little.

It was amazing how this rappelling was similar to meditation. You had to concentrate and focus—relax if you could, and be very present in your body as you descended. The net result was extreme clarity, lucidity, and wakefulness—together with a giddiness and a camaraderie shared by all the men who climbed together.

Coby made some more Turkish coffee, and Ohad handed me half of a large bagel together with a salt-spice mixture to dip it into. Then he gave me part of his hard-boiled egg. I took my first bite and my taste buds exploded, setting off a chain reaction throughout my senses.

"This is great!" I told Ohad and just about anyone else who would listen.

We started the third and, I hoped, last climb down. I watched Zac's eyes get bigger and bigger as he let out more and more rope.

"Oh, wow!" Zac said. "This one is over eighty meters!"

Then Ohad looked at me and said, "Eighty meters! What do you think, Bill?"

"I don't care," I said. "Anything over two meters is a lot for me—fifty meters or eighty meters, what's the difference?"

They all laughed.

"Bill, you're next," Zac said.

"Okay," I replied. Actually, I was happy to get it over with. Zac tied an extra loop around my waist while Coby gave me his gloves so that I wouldn't burn my hands again. Then, just before I went over the edge, Zac gave me one of the backpacks to carry down. And even though it was one of the smaller ones, it was a sign that they trusted me—to carry my own weight and pack extra gear.

They all crowded around to take my picture as I rappelled the last and highest of the cliffs—over eighty meters. A few meters over the edge, Savyon said, "Bill, look up."

I looked up into the camera and tried to give them a relaxed, joyful smile.

"Bill, let go of the ropes," they said. "Zac has you covered."

I let go of the ropes and put my arms straight out like a bird soaring or perhaps even Jesus on the cross.

"Are you scared?" someone asked.

"Totally!" I said just as Savyon snapped the picture, and they all burst into laughter.

As I descended, the rope ran through my right hand, but this time—instead of burning the flesh on my fingers away—the glove shielded me. I stopped three times on my way down so that I could look down and around. I still wasn't exactly joyful—but now at least I could stop, look, and relax a bit. Still I had to fight to be present with what was before me, because in the depths of my mind, the fear and anxiety wanted to push me through the experience and get it over with as quickly as possible.

You'll be able to relax then, the fear said.

But that's just a trap and a lie. Too much of my life has been lived that way, and I see it in others—this idea that *if I can just get through what's happening now, then in the future I will be able to relax, enjoy, and be present.* But somehow that future of relaxing and presence never seems to arrive. How often I've pushed myself through till the end of things. For example, when my girlfriend wants to talk about difficult emotions, I want it to be over.

"Is ten minutes okay?" I ask—because I know I can endure ten minutes.

But she doesn't want endurance; she wants relating, and relating to what's in front of you is killed when you are busy waiting for it to be over. Life becomes a sort of hell when lived like this—a place where we're tortured in small ways throughout the day. We endure the tortures, hoping all the while that they will end. If we sense they won't end, then we just avoid the torturing present until we don't meet the life we're given with spiritual presence and an open heart. Instead, we kill it through that avoidance, and everyone we meet and know loses—especially those we love.

Whether it's climbing down a cliff or talking with your mate or dealing with all the relating (both animate and inanimate) that comes up throughout the day, being present with it is a way to make hell into heaven. "The kingdom of heaven is spread out upon the earth, but men do not see it" (page 65, vs. 113). Jesus said in the Gospel of Thomas.

As I scaled closer to the bottom, I relaxed; but during the last thirty meters, the rope that supported me creaked as I descended. What if something went wrong?

"You have to trust the equipment," Eli said.

Zac had even shown me where each sixteen-hundred-shekel (four-hundred-dollar) rope had a name and a number stamped on it.

"The person checks each inch of rope as it comes off the line," he said. "That's why they're so expensive, and that's why a name is on each one—*we* know who to go to if there is a problem with the rope."

We all have an edge, and at the edge of who we are, there is a rope we can throw down, and we can descend if we want to. That's why I came to the desert: I wanted to descend more deeply into that which was unknown to me—and yet had controlled me because I was avoiding it.

You see, the secret is that we carry that unknown with us wherever we go. It comes up in the middle of a conversation with our mates, or when rappelling a cliff, or a thousand times during the day. If we avoid this edge and its unknown, our life becomes filled with blind spots—times when we are anxiously waiting for the unknown to pass. It's then that we may turn on the television or drink alcohol or take drugs or read a book or do any one of a thousand things to avoid this unknown that makes up much of our life. It is a life of desperate avoidance, or "quiet desperation," as Thoreau called it; a life of "the spiritually dead," as Jesus called it.

We can use anything to keep us out of the unknown, but if you want to know God fully, you must go there. For what is God, if not mostly that which is beyond what we know? Many religious people, evangelists, scholars, and mystics go to the edge, and then they use the Scriptures or their knowledge and concepts of God to keep them from going over the edge into the unknown God. Of course, God can never be fully known, and that's why his face can never be seen. But it is an act of faith, of true and deep love, to let go and fall into the face of God.

"It's so beautiful," Ohad had said, "that I just want to jump in and go toward it."

I am just a human being who prays for the guidance and the courage to jump in, to go toward God, to die into God. Whenever I jump, for a moment I am free in eternity. But then, since I am human, I land. There I build a dwelling, a house and a life for a while until my edge becomes apparent once more, and then it is time to jump again into that holy mystery. But I don't jump, because I am afraid—and I don't want to die. But then I remember the most valuable lesson a human being can learn: as I am falling, I will be falling into the face of God, and by losing my life in this way, I will actually save it.

day 24

I'm angry and tired.

"When can I rest?" I shout at God. "When does it end? When is it over?"

"The Son of Man has nowhere to lay His head," Jesus said (Matthew 8:20 NASB). For a moment this only adds to my thoughts and feelings of exhaustion and fear. But then I remember, this is why I came to the desert . . . for there is no deep rest as long as we are separate from God and the kingdom. To be "one with God," as Jesus said. "To see the beautiful and go toward it," as Ohad said. To smile and say, "Enjoy the day," as Eli said. These are all ways to let go and be with God, and that's why I came to the desert.

It's late evening, and the wind is gusting as heavily as I've seen it since I've been here. I'm sitting under my mosquito net, and the sand comes hurling through the net. Luckily, in this desert, it's mostly rock—otherwise, I'm sure this would be a blinding sandstorm.

Right now I feel the way I did when I was rappelling the cliff. I wish it were over and I was home. I'm starting to learn in my meditation that when I want my meditation to be over, it's often because something I've been avoiding is making its way through my unconscious to my conscious. It's a vague sense of discomfort, and I'm beginning to see how much of my life has been controlled by it—and not by me.

It was through my mother that I first encountered God. It was through her love that I felt the blessing that is inherent in love and, in a very real way, even in life. When she died and left me, a twelve-year-old boy, she left me with a secret that no one else understood. It was a secret she and I shared, often felt and experienced—but rarely spoke about. The secret is that even though no one has ever seen the face of God, when two people come together in love and a deep relationship with God, they see God's face in each other. That's why it is so hard when someone we love dies—one of God's faces has died.

In my meditation, while the wind gusted and the moon began to show, I fidgeted.

Then it came.

I began to hear a song over and over again in my head. It was the song that had been playing on the radio the day my mother died. I began to cry, then sob, then wail like a wounded animal. For nearly an hour I wailed. And I saw the darkness of that basement where I lived after my mother died. I saw my hands reaching out toward . . . more darkness. I wailed about having my love source taken away. I wailed at having my heart ripped out. Thirty years later I wailed.

As I wept, I sensed the love I'd lost and reached out with my hands to hold on to this love—but there was nothing to grab on to.

I cried more and then looked up at the night sky. The first and brightest star was out. It was so beautiful and bright that I reached out to grab it—but it was too far away.

Then a pervasive love from within me emerged. I even tried to grasp it, but as I closed around it, all that was caught in my grasp was my own tension.

Then I realized once again that love is uncapturable. It cannot be kept. It cannot be secured. It cannot be caught by any of my thinking, feeling, emoting, or bodily cravings; it can be expressed through them but neither captured nor conjured by them. But what's the point of trying to manipulate love anyway? It *can't* be manipulated by me, although *I can be manipulated and changed by it.*

As I let go of my posturing, my creative thoughts, my feelings, and my bodily attempts at holding love, it arises naturally; it is me, and it is all around me. That's why I came to the desert: so I could wail without interruption—and love without interruption.

day 25

I had my first dream about Dave last night. He looked good: solid and clear. We visited different places together and went to see different people he knew. I told Dave that I had seen his dad earlier in the dream.

"My dad's here?" he asked excitedly.

He found his dad and gave him a big hug. His dad was wearing a uniform and was going down into an underground garage. He looked like Gene, the guy who repairs my golf clubs. Gene is a kind, hardworking man who keeps his house meticulous and whose effect is a bit flat. But he and his wife are the type of honest, hardworking people we depend on.

In the dream, Dave went to the grade school where he taught, and his commanding presence came out. He puffed up his chest like a conquering general as he pushed open the school doors. We went into the gym, and all the middle schoolers asked, "How are you, Mr. Dahlia?" They were fond of him.

Dave told me not to squander my time in the desert. He said he was doing well—and I felt no need to ask him about his death. I told Dave several times he needed to see his mother, but that didn't seem foremost in his mind, so we didn't go. Then I woke up from that dream (but still dreaming) on the steps of the church down the block from where Dave and I and four other people had lived. There were police at the house where we had lived. It didn't look the same. A TV evangelist, who sounded like Reverend Ike, was talking with cops about a crime.

Now that I filled in the water hole, the bees are gone and the geckos are back. I watched a large one (a male?) sneak up on a small one (a female?). Part of me hoped they'd fight or mate because it would give me something to watch and pass the time.

I put two old tuna cans filled with water out for the bees because they were constantly coming by and searching for water. When I checked the cans a few hours later, there were four dead bees in one. Why? Was it food-poisoned remnants of old tuna? Or was it the small amount of oil that was still in the can? When I checked back later, the dead bees were gone. Who ate them?

I am very tired—probably the result of the "rappelling" day. I just want to lie on a couch, watch TV, and order a pizza—a deep-dish. I'm very aware today, so aware I can't stand it. I suppose the resistance means there is something I don't want to be aware of. Like Jesus and the rich man. The rich man was aware of much and wanted to follow Jesus, but he resisted giving up one final thing and the thing he held most dear—his money. Since I'm poor, I must be holding on to something else.

After I hit bottom for the last time on our descent down the cliffs the other day, I remembered that it was the Sabbath—and yet they were all climbing.

"Aren't you guys supposed to be resting?" I asked. "You know—keeping the Sabbath day holy or something like that?"

"This is where and how we cleanse our spirits," Zac said.

"This is my church," Eli said, raising his arms and acknowledging nature. "This is my church, where I heal my hurts." Then he got very serious and walked over—closer to me. "It's about being simple," he continued. "Just being a human being. But no one wants to be a human being—they all want to be original, but since they're trying to be original, they can't be.

"Did I just make sense?" he asked me.

"Totally," I said. "To be original, all you need to do is be yourself. You're the only Eli there will ever be, so if you're who Eli was meant to be, you are unique and original."

Everyone collected at the bottom of the last cliff. They all seemed so happy, centered, and clear. I wondered how much of this clarity, this joy, this focus and presence they carried back into life.

"It will be there for one day, maybe two," Savyon said. Then he shrugged his shoulders as if to say, "What can you do?"

That's why I came to the desert: so that the clarity and joy in my life can be taken with me wherever I may go; so that it doesn't depend on a place, an activity, a person, a thought, or an emotion. I wanted that free-spirited kind of joy that Jesus expressed when he said, "The son of man [or human being] hath not where to lay his head" (Matthew 8:20 KJV).

Jesus relied on no one or nothing or no thought for his human beingness. *He became a human being* instead of relying on something that gave him his human beingness. Thus he was free, and that is one of the examples he set for me. He showed me in a dramatic way that in order for me to become who I am, I must be crucified. Crucified on the cross, where the limited intersects with the limitless. I have been crucified, died, and been resurrected many times so far in the desert. For a moment I am eternity, then I am thrust back into my limitations. Then eternity comes again, then limitation again. The pain of crucifixion seems to come when eternity is captured by limitation. Or perhaps it is when limitation lets go into eternity?

Either way, I have come to my edge many times and let go and gone beyond. I've cried many times out of fear as I let go into eternity. Then I cry again as eternity becomes captured.

As I rappelled down each of the three rock-face walls, there were moments—eternal moments that tasted of hell—when I wanted it to be over. It was a constant letting go of fear and then fear that arose again and again—and so I let go again and again.

Jesus felt that same fear, and he was captured by it when he cried in the garden and sweated blood. But then he said, "Father, . . . not my will, but thine" (Luke 22:42 KJV), and he was back in eternity.

Jesus was caught many times by his limitations and his fear. "My God, my God, why have you forsaken me?" (Matthew 27:46) he said as he was dying. To be human means to have the courage to take your seat in eternity or being, while taking your stand in your humanity—your limitation. This was Jesus's greatest feat, the greatest miracle, the greatest realization he had: by being a human being, he had fulfilled every Scripture that was written and could ever be written.

"I have set you an example," he said. And what was he doing when he said that? Was he raising the dead? Was he making the blind see? Was he breaking bread and saying, "Drink my blood"? Was he dying for our sins?

No—none of those things. The most important thing Jesus did was wash another friend's feet. He was eternity humbling itself as a human being, and by doing this, he exalted and showed us what a true miracle is.

After I said good-bye to Eli, he pointed at his father, who was laughing while he slid down a dry stone waterfall.

"That's why I'm crazy about him," he said. "He's just like a child."

Zac, Mayer, and I hiked the last one and a half miles down a rocky hillside to the Dead Sea. Mayer said, "I no speak English," so I said to Zac, "Please tell Mayer it's obvious he's a good man, and both his sons, Eli and Ohad, are good men too."

Zac translated, and Mayer smiled back at me with a joy that translated into any language.

"You will remember this day," Zac said, "as being one of the great days of your life."

"You're right," I said. "It is one of the great days of my life."

Then we came to a drop-off of about sixty feet. Zac wanted to climb down, and as we got halfway down, there was no way to go the final thirty feet.

"There's a path along the hill up there," I said, having seen it earlier. It looked like a goat trail but was marked with stones as the bedouins do. We ended up taking *my way* the rest of the way down, and I felt good about the fact that I had spotted the path before they did.

"I will go home," Zac said, "but I won't really talk about what happened here. They wouldn't understand—they don't understand what or why.

"Most people want material things," he continued. "But they will die poor—even the ones with money will die poor."

By the time Zac and Mayer dropped me off near my tent, it was dark. I was exhausted, but as tired as I was, I couldn't resist going back out to the plateau to stand in the gusty winds as I looked up at the stars.

"Hoo-ah! Hoo-ah! Hoo-ah!" I shouted into the night. I felt clear and open. Then I started talking out loud to God.

"I still don't know why I'm here," I said. "But the best answer I have is *that I am here.*

"I've seen a lot of pain and suffering in my time," I continued. "A lot of it, you had something to do with. I hated you a lot for the things you did. But I love you—I love you because what you are moves through me.

"I really wish I could have seen Jesus in his glory. I know he's something now, but to have seen him do his thing in a body—

that would have been something! I suppose I should thank you
for not letting me kill myself like Dave did . . .

"Thanks," I said.

"Thanks for letting me live; I mean, if I would have ended it
back then—twenty years ago—life and I wouldn't have parted
on good terms. And then I never would have wanted to come
back here. I still don't necessarily want to come back . . .

"I would like to live a long life, if that's okay. And I guess if
you do find yourself in a fix down here, maybe I'd help you out!"
I said sarcastically. "You know, come down here and set the
record straight.

"I would like to make a living at writing, if that's okay, and
I'd like to help people—you know I like doing that . . .

"And a woman . . . help me to know if Bonnie's the one or not.

"And thank you for a very full day."

I walked back to my tent, wiped my body down, and ate a
can of tuna fish with a whole-wheat pita. Then I fell asleep.

day 26

Thirty-five minutes into my meditation, I just couldn't take it. The psychological and spiritual pain and bodily sensations were too much, and I was tired of it. I opened my eyes and punched my mosquito net three times.

"Why do I have to put up with all this damn pain? I didn't ask to be here. I don't know one freakin' person on this planet who asked to be here. How could we ask if we hadn't been created yet? Why do you do this to me and every other human being? Oh yeah, I know about all that philosophical stuff—how 'I'm the cause of much of my pain.' But what do you expect? You put us here and never tell us anything. You never tell us anything!

"Oh," I said, pointing to the Bible, "that's supposed to tell us something? All that tells us is that if we do something you don't like, you're going to punish us. And even now—my being angry at you—like I'm not supposed to get angry at you or swear at you or you'll what? You'll hurt me or threaten me? You sound like my father. If I got angry at him, he'd hit me or threaten to hit me unless I shut up.

"Just tell me! Just tell me why I'm here! Don't give me this love talk—like I'm supposed to always relax into your love and love makes it all okay!

"Just talk to me! Come right here. Right now. Right in front of my face and talk to me!"

I stopped my tirade and looked at my surroundings. All I saw were nature and space.

"No," I said, shaking my head, "I don't want you talking to me through your creation. I want you to come here right now and just friggin' . . . talk to me!

"I don't believe this—you put us here for what? You watch us suffer and you made us—and made life this way—and you can't even come here and tell me why? Just tell my why! Just come and tell me!" I shouted out into the desert.

"I don't want all that philosophical crap from other people. I don't want to hear what a guy said two thousand years ago! What about now? You owe it to us to at least tell us face-to-face—why? Why do you put us through this? I want to know now!" I stopped and waited for an answer.

The desert was silent, except for the buzzing of a bee, the call of a distant bird, and the wind.

"Damn," I said, getting off my meditation cushion. "I'm going to make myself a cup of coffee."

Whenever you put anyone on a pedestal, whether it's Jesus or someone you know, it's not because you honor them. No, mostly you put them on a pedestal above you because you think you're trash and they aren't. If you really loved yourself *and* admired them, you'd shake their hand and tell them face-to-face.

When I emerged from my mosquito net after my angry prayer and outburst, my surroundings seemed so beautiful and calm that I had to smile. In a relationship, forgiveness goes both ways, and when "the air has been cleared," there is no longer an obstruction; both parties can now smile and see why they loved each other in the first place.

I've noticed that animals talk a lot to each other. I will hear a gecko talking to a gecko on the other side of the canyon with his "popping" sounds. Or a bird will be talking to another bird way far away, saying, "R-We-Ree?"

Another bird says, "Deeep," in a high-pitched way, and still another says, "Dorthia" or something—I haven't totally figured it out yet.

I also saw two black beetles meet face-to-face. I bet they were talking too.

As I'm here, I try not to "look" at myself "being here." Of course, it happens, but I let go of that "looking" and just come back to what I'm doing. On the flight home or after I'm home, I can look back and reflect. But now it's important for me to just sit, just see, just sleep, just write, just pray, and just be.

Like Moses, I desire to see the face of God that is the present

in which I live. But I would cease to have that "real" life if I
stepped out of it in order to see it. Even then I would see only
the back of the "present" as it has already passed. I would see only
the past—the wake of God—and cease living in the present or
God's presence.

"The kingdom of Heaven is spread out upon the earth, but
men do not see it" (page 65, vs. 113), Jesus said in the Gospel
of Thomas.

You can never see it—you can only be it. And once you are
being it, then you can see it in whatever you look at.

My prayer and meditation time/experience has changed/taken
a big turn. I am experiencing the spaciousness and Being that I
felt deeply with Lama Chokyi Nyima at the Dzogchen retreat
last year.

When I am in this space, my body no longer hurts so much,
and when it does, it seems to release or disperse its pain/tension
into the space around it. I can sit longer then. When I looked
down at my watch to see how long it had been (I figured an hour
and fifteen minutes or more), the clock said only fifteen minutes!
As I looked closer, I saw that my watch had stopped. I laughed
and clapped, saying "good one" to the universe for "stopping" time
when I was in a "timeless" place of prayer. It was a good joke.

In my meditation I felt very spacious, and again I experienced
the presence of my friend Dave. On the way to the hospital,

while in the back of the police car, Dave turned to me and said, "I'm sorry, Bill."

He said he was sorry because his soul, which was as large as just about any I've met, knew that his time was up and that he was leaving me and that we would not grow old as friends, talking about how I ate whole chickens while rocking in the rocking chair or about the time he stole the presidents. Oh? I didn't tell you about how he stole the presidents? About the greatest heist outside the Old West? Well, here goes.

Dave Dahlia dated my sister twenty-three years ago in the small town of Richland Center, Wisconsin. She was a librarian at the middle school. Every so often Dave would substitute there, and whenever he visited my sister in the library, he'd look around at the walls, where framed paintings of the first thirty-six presidents hung.

"Miss Elliott," he'd goad her, "how can you have these guys on the wall? Most of them were crooks! Especially that guy!" And Dave would point to Richard Nixon.

"Did you know he was a Quaker, Miss Elliott?

"What kind of example are you giving the youth of America!" he'd say, slamming his fist on her desk. This went on every time he visited her, and a few months later, after she broke up with Dave, she came into school one day, looked up on the wall, and *they were gone!* All thirty-six presidents, paintings and frames— gone! All that was left were thirty-six spots where the paint had not faded over the years—and a single, red dahlia on the librarian's desk. The calling card of Dave Dahlia.

Just then the principal came in. "Don't worry, Liz," he said. "I've already called the police!" Then, shaking his head, he wondered out loud, "Who would take the presidents?"

The principal looked at my sister. She gulped but never told anyone who took the presidents.

"Bill!" Dave said ecstatically. "You should have seen me! I took a screwdriver and pried open the window. It was easy. The hardest part was carrying all thirty-six presidents home with me at three o'clock in the morning.

"The frames were the bulkiest part," Dave added.

Dave took all the presidents to Madison, Wisconsin, where he pinned them up on Laundromat walls, co-op bulletin boards, and street kiosks. Except for one president—Richard Nixon.

"This is for you, Wonder Brother," Dave said.

I looked at Nixon's face.

"Turn it over," Dave said.

I turned it over, and on the back side was Nixon's biography; underneath the category "Religion," it said, "Quaker."

I was driving my car a little over a year ago when my cell phone rang. It was my friend Roger.

"Well, our friend followed through with his plan," he said. "Dave killed himself—exactly like he said he would. He drove over to the college parking lot at about three in the morning and taped a hose to his exhaust pipe with the duct tape."

I pulled over on the side of the road. I pounded my fist into the dashboard and said, "No!" Then I got out of my car and sat by a field, even though I never cared much for nature. It's not that I dislike nature; it's just that it doesn't turn me on like it did Dave or some people I know. But as I sat there in the field, I suddenly felt Dave's presence, and then the whole field and all the trees—everything that was natural—glowed. I stared at the living luminosity with more than my eyes, and *I knew* it was Dave's good-bye present to me.

"See that, Bill?" I could feel him say. "That's why I love the outdoors."

My meditations are "just sitting" now. They are very pleasurable and interesting. My butt hurts, though—right where it meets my spine. It feels as if a horse kicked me there.

People I know who have died sometimes "visit me" in my sittings. For example, once when I was meditating, I let go and felt a place open in my upper chest. It was a place I remembered closing when my grandmother died when I was nine. As it opened, I heard her call my name. She told me she loved me. I had loved her very much, and it hurt deeply when she died. But now many of those places I had held closed were being hollowed out and opened, revealing the love that had long been hidden for someone who's now gone.

"I am willing to act like a fool in order to show my joy in the LORD."
—David to his wife, 2 Samuel 6:21 NLT

I boiled some noodles and ate them as the wind was *really* blowing. Then I went into my tent and undressed. Since I had extra water, I decided to wash and went back outside naked except for sandals. I soaped up my body and poured two pitchers of water over my head, then dried off in the desert night while looking up at the moon—it looked full. Then I started to dance while the wind blew. I started to sing, "I am doing the . . ."

Then I stopped singing. *What dance am I doing?* I danced and watched myself. *I'm dancing like a palm tree blowing in the wind.*

"I am doing the palm tree dance," I sang, "the palm tree dance . . . the palm tree dance.

"I am doing the palm tree dance . . ." And then it dawned on me that I was dancing in the Judean desert at night—*naked*. So I changed songs.

"I am dancing naked in the desert—the desert," I sang while holding the shampoo bottle in my left hand and the pee bottle in my right. "I'm dancing naked in the desert—the desert."

Then I stopped and started another conversation with God.

"Is it okay if I have fun?" I asked.

"Thank you for another full day," I said, "and for letting me say the things I did. It helped a lot . . .

"I'm going to bed."

day 27

My energy is low. I don't have much to say. This canyon is filled with caves of many sizes. In 1948 at Qumran and in 1945 at Nag Hammadi, scrolls were found in caves by accident. I walked among the caves today, but I didn't find any scrolls.

Above me in the cave, I heard the "clucking" and "squeaking" sounds that geckos make when they are having a confrontation. All of a sudden one fell from the ceiling onto the stone floor with a loud *splat*. I looked out my mosquito net, concerned, but the gecko just hugged a rock for a while and then slowly moved away.

In my meditation/prayer, I began to gag, and just trusted the wisdom of God. I gagged until I bent over and coughed deeply as if to expel an evil spirit. Then I gasped for a while as though I had just been born, like a baby learning how the lungs worked.

The breath is holy. In Aramaic (the language Jesus spoke) and

Hebrew, the word for both "breath" and "spirit" is the same—
ruach. So whenever Jesus said, "Holy Spirit," he just as easily
could have meant Holy Breath. That's why John 20:22 says, "He
breathed on them and said, 'Receive the Holy Spirit.'"

That's also why when people try to hide the truth of how
they feel, they often do it by restricting their breath, which
simultaneously paralyzes their spirit of truth.

Later in my meditation, the impermanence of all things—
especially *my impermanence* and all that happens in me—was so
clear. Then I thought of my brothers and sisters all getting older,
and how they will start to die soon—one by one. I love them so
much. They are a part of me, and when they die, I will no longer
have them to be with, to find security with and enjoy. I will have
memories as I let go of them, and I will have the spaces of love
within me that they occupied, but the hardest thing will be to
feel that space of love without anything to hold on to.

We humans like to hold as we love, and that's why experiencing God's presence is hard—because God is a love that cannot be held; it is intangible. It is only through another that
God's love can be held; it is a tangible love and occurs when two
people reach out or grow roots toward each other and touch
each other within love. Eventually those who touch us in this
way die—and we are left with arms open, feeling as though the
other is no longer reaching out toward us. So it is a terrible
thing to realize, in the very core of who I am, that they will all
leave me and I will lose that tangible touch of love.

I know many people who *say* they know that everyone dies,
but I get the impression that it is just a shallow thought for
them and not a living reality and experience they carry with
them. The terrible thing about death is that it will end the lives

of the people you love. The good thing about death is if you pay attention to it, it can add more life to your life by giving you the strength to overcome the fears that kill life before your life is over. I hope my love for those I love, and my knowing that our time together is limited, will overpower any fear I have of telling them how I feel.

It was super windy again tonight. I went out under the stars and full moon on the Fourth of July. It was during Passover, the Jewish version of the Fourth of July, that Jesus conducted his famous temple incident two thousand years ago.

I stood under a full moon, and I began another conversation.

"I have this fear in me now," I said, "that I could die at any time. That any little thing I do may cause my death. I might get bitten by a snake, or trip and bump my head against a rock, or fall off a cliff, or have a heart attack—anything can happen here. Or I can go home, die in a car crash, have a heart attack— you get the picture . . ."

I felt so vulnerable. My mortality was not just staring me in my face—*it was my face.*

"How easy it is to die!" I said softly, as the meaning went out from and more deeply into me at the same time. Then I thought about my family and friends again. They were in the same boat—even if they didn't realize it. That's the reason I wanted to jump off the edge. I wanted to get it over with. I'd rather die now by my own choosing than live with the anxiety of death always hanging over me. Just like when I was rappelling the cliff, I wanted to get to the bottom and end the fear.

But I don't kill myself or rush to the end of my life, even though I try to avoid my life by killing it in small ways when it gets to be too much, or when I'm so alive that it's painful to be that aware.

"Why can't I just focus on what a great experience it is to be alive?" I said to God. "Why can't I just enjoy the experience?"

Then I paused as I looked around the dark, shadowy desert—illuminated in places by the full moon.

"Actually," I said, a bit giddy and excited, "this is an amazing thing. What an amazing thing! This life is like being on an exciting ride at an amusement park. You get on, you start, and then there are scary parts, and you don't yell, 'Stop the ride; I want to get off!' That's partly why you get on the ride—to get scared and excited."

All of a sudden I saw my whole life as an experience, as though I were some alien coming to earth, saying, "Let's try that one!"

I looked up at the full moon. They say people get crazier on the full moon; that's where *lunatic* and *loony* come from, the word *lunar*. I suddenly laughed, and as I did, I saw myself as loony, which made me laugh more. Then I walked back to my tent and tried to sleep. But the winds were so strong that I lay awake, half expecting my tent to be ripped apart at any moment.

day 28

I woke up late—it was hot.

Of course it's hot! I thought as I looked at my clock. *It's 8:00 a.m.!*

I—my body and mind—felt heavy. I didn't want to get up, but as I sat up, I saw a small platoon of red ants stealing my food.

"Uh-oh!" I said. I immediately started to eliminate them. I never did find out how they got into my tent. After I exited my tent, I duct-taped down the flaps—covering any holes.

That's another reason I came to the desert—I wanted to cover any holes, those places where my life was leaking out, and experience my life as fully as possible. Jesus said, "I've come to bring you life in full!" (see John 10:10). And if you remember, he said that after being in the desert. It helps me to remember that while Jesus was in the desert, he wasn't exactly partying it up. He was being tempted by his demons—just as I am by mine. In the desert you can see your demons more clearly. There aren't many places they can hide. Back in the city the demons hide in everything from television to Dove Bars, from women you want to men you want to be like. It's in the mirror when you get up; it's in the midday cup of coffee; it's in the way I look at people as they look at me. Whether it's judgment of others, self-criticism, fear, or just plain avoidance, barely any moment completely escapes the infiltration of our demons.

I came to the desert so that the demons didn't have so many places to hide. And I came to find out their names. Often before Jesus removed demons from people, he asked the demon its name. You name something after you know it. Naming and knowing give you power.

That's why I came to the desert—to name and know my demons in the silence of the desert.

I also came to the desert in order to *stop* giving God names—because *naming something gives you power over it.*

And as the early Jews knew, to name God gave man a power that came from the mistaken notion that he actually knew God—and that power is exactly the thing that separates a human being from the Supreme Being.

Have you ever noticed how few people actually look at you—really look at you as though they are really there, really present?

Well, it's usually because there's something they're avoiding. Often something happening now is reflecting off something that happened before—and since they are avoiding any "before," they have to avoid now. The greatest miracle that

Jesus ever performed was being alive now. He was so alive, he burned a Presence of Now so intense that those who had made their dwelling in a place of the past either followed him or feared him. Those who feared him killed him.

That's why I went to the desert—to follow the example of Jesus and allow the miracle to happen, to live the miracle by facing the parts of me that fear the only life worth living.

In my morning prayer/meditation, I cried bunches. I cried for how much I love my family and people I know. Did you ever love someone so much that you had to cry?

Toward the end of my meditation, so many images and desires came and went. The anticipation of being done with my forty days. The faces of my many friends and family seen through a more deeply found self and joy. And the sound of Tibetan mantras along with visions of a serene monk's face mouthing holy words even while dying at the hands of the Chinese. Whatever and whomever they were, I let them go; consequently, they stayed only as long as they needed to.

And toward the last minutes of my prayer, while I cried, my cries began to slowly change into laughter. Instead of crying over the tragic experiences of my life, I was now laughing at them; laughing as though I was now at a different point on the scary ride at the amusement park. I laughed at the excitement of it, and I laughed at myself and how afraid and serious I had been only moments before. Then I heard his laugh—the spine-tingling laugh I heard more than seventeen years ago and never forgot.

I had been traveling through a small, rural Tibetan village in

Nepal, and while I waited for a bus, I heard from behind me a slow-starting but increasingly intense laugh.

"Heeee . . . Heee . . . Heee . . . ," it began.

I turned to see a Tibetan man in ragged clothes. He was reclined on a bench, looking every bit as comfortable as a man at home in his castle—lounging on *his couch*.

"Heee, Heee, Heee . . . ," he continued. He looked at me—*and through me*. I suddenly felt self-conscious, sort of embarrassed—like the emperor in *The Emperor's New Clothes*—standing before the innocent, uncensored mouthpiece for the naked Truth.

"What are you laughing at?" I asked—afraid of the answer I knew was coming.

"You!" he said as coolly and directly as any gunfighter in the Old West.

The hair stood up on my neck. I started talking to him and found that he was actually very gentle and his English was perfect. When I gave him my name, he wrote it down again in perfect English.

What was a Tibetan man, who was dressed in rags and who spoke and wrote perfect English, doing looking like some mentally ill beggar?

I told him about my college thesis, which was titled "A Philosophical and Dialectical Inquiry into the Major Religions of the Katmandu Valley." My thesis really was a ruse to get me over to Nepal so that I could find somebody who knew what was going on in life, because I sure hadn't found anyone back home who knew.

He asked to see the list of questions I asked each wise person I found. He said he would answer them the next day.

But I never went back to see him, and I never saw him again.

I've always regretted that. And even now, while out here in the desert, I still remember that laugh—a laugh that seemed to come out of eternity itself, exposing everything false in me. With a laugh like that, I wondered, was he crazy or enlightened?

I saw the beautiful black-and-white bird again. He looked very elegant, very dignified. He's mostly black, with a touch of white; it makes him look like he's wearing a very tasteful but low-key tuxedo.

"You're related to the penguin," I said to him. He just looked away, as though he didn't know what I was talking about.

"You are," I said. "You're related to the penguin—you kind of look like one, but . . ."

And then, as though insulted, he gathered himself together and, in a huff, flew away.

He didn't let me finish. It's too bad, because I was about to say that he was much thinner than a penguin and much more regal.

In my prayer times, I see old friends. Many of them are people I've known who have died. They smile at me as though they are reintroducing me to a deeper part of our relationship—a part I had forgotten. They are gatekeepers and guardians of those special places where we touched one another, places they helped open.

For example, my old friend Len, who died in a tragic car

accident, came clearly to me—and he was his happy, delightful, carefree self.

"Billeee, Billeee, Billeee!" I heard him say, and as he appeared I could feel the "titillation" of life. That delightful part of life that is such a "fine" part of us it's hard to just be it and relax. But Len relaxed in his titillation, delight, and sexuality so much that it was in his eyes whenever you looked at him. Len loved life; he was like the real Zorba the Greek, the friend of Nikos Kazensakis who said, "Men like me should live a thousand years!"

I first met Len while pumping iron. Back then I had a habit of asking other weight lifters what they thought the meaning of life was. Mostly I got "What?" or "Huh?" in response. But when I asked Len, he said, "Well, Socrates thought . . . ," and that was the beginning of a kindred relationship. You see, Len and I shared a secret, and we shared it with each other. It was a secret that cannot be told to another—not because of secrecy, but because of its nature. Some call this secret a connection, but it is within this connection that the secret is revealed. Len and I would sit in coffee shops, look out the window, and talk about life in such a way that *the secret would naturally arise.*

"Bill," Len once said, "I work with some people who just care about money and crap. That's all they care about—*crap!* What we talk about is real, what we try to live is real . . ." And then he would look at me and add, "I look so forward to talking with you about this stuff. It really makes my day. I just eat it up when we sit here like this. My other friends aren't like this."

Len and I occasionally went to bars, and while drinking beer we'd simultaneously flex our pectorals—making them go up and down—laughing so hard we'd just about puke.

Not long before Len died, he took up dancing and playing

the saxophone and decided to sell his business. Then one day, he and three other businessmen drove their vintage Mercedes down to a Chicago Bulls game. The car broke down, and while they waited on the side of the highway for a tow truck, a semi-truck driver fell asleep at the wheel, drove onto the shoulder, and killed all four of them as they sat in the car.

Anyway, today Len appeared to me in my meditation just as I entered a place in my soul that was semiclosed. First, I cried at his memory, but then as the grief passed, I was left with the love.

"Let's dance, Billeee!" Len said, standing in the midst of my being. Delightful energy flooded into me and titillated me to the point where I almost pushed it away. But then he said again, "Let's dance, Billeee!"

And as he smiled and danced, my soul smiled and danced— and relaxed into places I had long forgotten.

After Len died, I found out the name of the truck driver who fell asleep at the wheel and slammed into Len's car. I got his phone number from information and called. His son answered and said that his father couldn't come to the phone.

"I was a friend of one of the men who died in the accident," I said. "My friend's name was Len, and Len was the kind of guy who would have forgiven your father. Len would have wanted your father to not feel guilty about what happened and to go on and enjoy his life. So I just hope you tell your father I called and that Len would have forgiven him."

As my meditation ended, I heard sounds I had not heard before. I opened my eyes and saw a herd of desert deer—ibex—coming over the ridge and into my canyon. They ate brush as they got closer. I watched them for twenty minutes. I got up slowly and moved closer by hiding behind rocks. I felt like an ancient hunter stalking wild game, but I had no intent to harm, only to watch. In order to get even closer, I lay on a rock and tried to blend in like a chameleon. I tried to be still and heavy—without a lot of quickness in mental or bodily energy. I even thought of taking off my shorts because they made noise as I moved—but Ya'el was supposed to bring my weekly supply of water today, and I didn't want to be caught in my B-day suit. After about ten minutes, one deer must have smelled me, because it looked up and made a sound. Then I could hear (but not see) what sounded like the head male ibex snorting and stamping his hoof. He was trying to flush me out, but I kept perfectly still.

Just then I heard the sound of a car pulling up, and someone beeped the horn. Then I heard a man talking, and when I climbed out of my cave and went up to the plateau, the bedouin were there.

"We brought your water," a man said. "Do you remember me?"

"Of course," I said as I realized that it was Yusuf, his brother, and another man. There was still someone seated in their truck—a four-wheel-drive Subaru.

"Is it okay if my wife comes down?" Yusuf asked.

"Yes—please," I said.

"You have tea? Cups?" Yusuf asked.

"Yes," I said, suddenly remembering the bedouin system of inviting guests for tea.

"I have tea—come, come," I said.

"We brought tea and a pot," Yusuf said.

I ran into my tent and got whatever I could offer them. Some banana chips, cashews, and almonds.

"This is your food?" Yusuf said, referring to my limited supply of food for forty days.

"No—it's okay," I insisted. "Ya'el has been bringing me food."

We were seated in a circle. They especially liked the banana chips and the cashews. Then Yusuf's wife got up (she was seated across from him) and sat directly behind him so that I could no longer look directly at her.

"You like the desert?" he asked. But he asked it in such a way that I knew he was asking more than that. He was really asking, *How do you like my dwelling? How do you like* my *life?*

"I love it," I said.

Yusuf beamed.

"Years ago the bedouin lived in the desert," he said. "They had sheep, camel—and we felt very good in here," he said, placing his hand on his heart.

"But now we don't live in desert—we take money—and we don't feel so good in here," he said, again putting his hand on his heart.

Then Yusuf's brother pulled out a pack of cigarettes and offered me one. At first I said no, because I don't smoke, but then I felt a wish to take what was offered. So I took one and lit up, trying to look as natural as possible.

"You have cups?" Yusuf asked.

I stood up and gathered together the only four cups I had. They were thrown about and dirty, so I quickly washed them in a basin.

"You make fire?" Yusuf asked.

I was suddenly horrified. I didn't want to look like an idiot as I tried to make a fire, so I ran over behind my tent and came back with my stove.

"That no good," Yusuf said, so his nephew built a fire and began heating up the tea. After it was done, his nephew toasted some white bread on a hot rock. They handed me a piece.

"This is really good," I said.

"It is better to make—how you say, *flour* and water—and put on grill. Is that right? *Grill?*"

I tried to explain that a grill is for a barbeque and that he was really talking about a flat pan, but as often happened in our conversation, we just stopped and stared at each other—smiling.

"How much Tamir charge you for helping you?" Yusuf asked. I smiled uncomfortably, because it really wasn't his business.

He smiled again in a very curious way.

"How much?" he asked.

When I told him, he said, "This isn't right—why he need take money for this?"

I tried to explain that Tamir needed to make a living, too, but Yusuf didn't seem to understand that.

"Why does Tamir help you? For money or to help you?" Yusuf asked.

"Both," I said.

"No—this not good to take money. The bedouin way is if you need something, a bedouin will get on his camel and travel all night to get it for you. If you come to his tent, he will be so happy that you came that if he only have twenty sheep, he will kill one and make you food. If you ask to be part of his family, he will take you in right then—and *you will be as family.*"

Yusuf looked at me with his deep brown eyes. I didn't see

much deception (if any) in him. He was like Nathanael, in whom Jesus said there was "no guile" (John 1:47 KJV).

The bedouins all seemed that way: simple, innocent, and true.

"The bedouins are the most trustworthy people you'll ever meet," my friend Shahabuddin had told me back in the States.

"Taking money," Yusuf said, rubbing his forefinger and thumb together, "I think is no good."

Then I showed them my cave, and even his wife climbed down.

"She must be careful," Yusuf's brother said. "She is with child."

"But she is bedouin," Yusuf said proudly.

They stood staring at my cave and my mosquito net with big smiles.

"This is the best way to live!" Yusuf's brother said.

"You like it here?" Yusuf asked—again in a way that gave me *the feeling he was asking, How do you like living my life? Do you approve?*

"I like it very much," I said genuinely, while thinking he was lucky he hadn't stopped by the first ten days because he might not have liked my answer.

"We must go," he said. "I am so very happy that we got to visit you here—it make me very happy."

"Me too," I said. "Thank you so much."

They got into their truck and drove off, waving joyfully. Later, when I walked up the ridge to relieve myself, I looked around just in case—and there they were, seated on the edge of a cliff about three quarters of a mile away. They watched the moon come up over the Dead Sea, looking every bit a part of the land and one another.

day 29

I woke up and killed five or six ants in my tent. How do they get in? If I kill them, does their "ant family" say, "We'd better not go there anymore"?

There was one ant who was proudly running off with a single grain of couscous. He held it up like a trophy, as though he had just won the Stanley Cup. He was so thrilled that I didn't have the heart to smoosh him. Instead, I picked him up with the edge of a postcard and set him outside.

One more day and it's a ten-day countdown! Like the countdown to an Apollo launch. Now that the end is within reach, I think about it more—just like I thought about the bottom when I rappelled the cliff wall. If I ever rappel a cliff wall again, I will be happier about doing it. I will enjoy it even more and have less of me stuck in *fear* and *thoughts of finishing*. Instead, I'll relax into the thrill of it—and perhaps even the *love*? Is that what emerges when you finally begin to settle down and fear subsides? Is that what you begin to see and feel? *Love?*

Once my friend Henry fell in love.

"I noticed I started looking at myself in the mirror more," he said. "And I was kind of happy."

Years later, after not having seen him for a while, we stayed up all night talking and drinking coffee. After he went home, he called me. But before I tell you what he said, I have to tell you what Henry is like. Henry is a guy who doesn't like to say the word *love*.

"If you love someone," he once told me, "they know it, and you don't have to tell them."

I argued with him, told him that was not true and that he had to tell people he loved them—*actually say the words*. But Henry insisted he was right.

"They know," he said. "I don't have to tell them."

I always thought it was Henry's fear of vulnerability speaking that day—not his wisdom. He was too afraid to express how much people meant to him. So when he called me years later and said, "After our visit together, I noticed I was looking at myself in the mirror—kind of happy like I did when I was in love years ago . . ."

Then he paused, as though debating whether to go over the edge—*past his edge*. He took a deep breath and said, "I think I'm understanding more of what love is."

Henry was rappelling a cliff. It wasn't a cliff anyone else could see, but it was as unknown and dangerous to him as anything I have found here in the desert.

I've been thinking about my rappelling of the cliffs, and there is so much meaning there for me. While rappelling the first cliff,

I was very afraid and my awareness was very narrow. On the second cliff, I relaxed a bit and my view was wider. On the third cliff, I was the least afraid and my awareness was the widest of all. *And that was the key.* In my life, I've met people who are very narrow-minded, and it drives me nuts. But then I realized, *They're just on the first cliff of life, and that's why they're so narrow and afraid.* Other people may be more open, but that's just because they are on the second or third cliff of life. I don't necessarily believe in reincarnation, but when a person is relaxed, awake in the present, and not panicking, we call them an *old soul.* Because they're experts at life, they've rappelled each moment over and over again until they're relaxed and proficient at being present one moment at a time. And it's always changing, because sometimes when I'm interacting with people or with life, I'm the one on the last cliff and they're on the first, or I may be on the first cliff and they're on the last cliff—and if we're both on the same cliff, *well, let's just hope it's not the first cliff.*

And what if the Bible story of Adam and Eve is actually a story about being on the first cliff? What if it tells us how the first humans reacted by being afraid and then hiding from the Supreme Being after having their eyes opened? The Christians and Buddhists agree on this point: that all experiences are built upon the first experience—the experience of being separate from God and afraid. And they both agree on the solution: *the real and true experience of our oneness with the Supreme Being will dispel fear and ignorance.*

That's why I came to the desert—to return to my first experience of fear; to sit with that fear until my eyes, ears, and touch let go of their petrified hold on my being, revealing what has always been true.

I'm really sick of the food I brought. All I have left are mainly white rice noodles and some nuts and raisins. *I don't want to look at another raisin!* And the nuts are making me nuts! The white rice noodles are so pasty. It's like eating nothing that's good for you. So I'm depending on Ya'el or Tamir to drop off some tuna, granola, and whole-wheat pita bread. Today I ate only half a Clif Bar and a cup of soy milk.

I almost wish I would do another forty days in the desert someday because I'd know what to bring next time! In hindsight, it's easy to see where to improve things. And when this is over, I'll even be able to help people with *their* forty days in the desert. That's who Jesus was. He was the part of "us" at the end who came back to our beginning in order to teach us. "I am . . the Beginning and the End," he said (Revelation 22:13).

"You are in me, and I am in you," he said (John 14:20).

He came back in order to give us pointers, to show us how to improve. He showed us who and what we would become.

"You will do all I have done and more," he said (see John 14:12).

As I bowed down in prayer and conversation with God, I was filled with the realization of how completely we must love, and how little we must hold on within that love.

In my prayer/meditation, I feel a lot of "creative energy" coming through, and I am *getting pulled in* by it. I also feel a lot of "seeing people's *soul energy*"—and am *getting pulled in* by it also. What I mean by "getting pulled in" is that as human beings we have many different instincts, abilities, and modes of operating that are emotional, mental, sexual, and physical. If we get pulled in by these, our soul is controlled and hijacked by them. That is why it is best to *watch* and *be* in meditation practice. It's called "practice" because I'm practicing how to experience these tendencies or energies freely so that when they arise in the midst of life, they do not enslave me. If I am free of the compulsion to jump aboard now, I will be free to choose later.

day 30

At the moment, I'm eating a Clif Bar and drinking powdered soy milk that I added to water. The soy milk is more like soy powder floating in water, but after thirty days in the desert, it tastes pretty good. The Clif Bar is pretty decent. It's the chocolate espresso flavor. The "apricot," "chocolate chip-peanut butter," and "cookies & cream" were my favorite flavors, and I ate them all in the first two weeks. If I came to the desert again, that's one thing I'd do differently—bring more Clif Bars. When I first got here, there were some days I ate two a day. They're made from whole grains with brown rice syrup instead of sugar. They're pretty healthy and were invented by some dude while he lived in a garage twelve years ago. He named the Clif Bar after his father, Clif, whom he called "his childhood hero and companion throughout the Sierra Nevada mountains." How do I know so much about this Clif Bar guy? Because on every package of Clif Bars there's a little biography. And when you spend thirty days in the desert with only the Bible, you'll read anything else you can find—over and over again. I found a newspaper in the desert one day. I picked it up and tried to read it, but I think it was in Hebrew. I stared at it anyway—for a long time—because it was something different, and in the words of Bill Murray in *Groundhog Day*, "anything different is good!"

I dreamed about my mother twice last night. I usually dream about her once a year, so twice in one night is unique. I saw her face very clearly, more so than usual. In one dream she looked like she did when she died—midfifties, red hair. But in the second dream she was very ill, very old, and lying in bed. I was stroking her head, and her hair was thin and white. In the dream my breathing was very strained, as though I was so worried about her impending death that the intense fear was just pressing down on my chest. Then I saw a large stone block that had the word *FEAR* scrawled across it. In front of the block sat a man who was so immobile I didn't know if he was alive or even if he was a real person. He had blond hair.

I woke up from the dream to the sounds of multiple flocks of large crows squawking. They flew so close to my tent, I could hear their powerful wings pushing them through the friction-filled atmosphere. I thought for a moment that they were intending to land on my tent, and I even imagined them ripping it wide open with their powerful beaks.

I had to kill six or seven ants in my tent again. How are they getting in?

I haven't been eating much. My appetite is practically gone. I bet I have lost fifteen pounds so far. Probably twenty, by the time I leave. I wonder how much weight Jesus lost in the desert?

Boy! Today is Friday, the beginning of the weekend, and people are flocking to the desert. Actually, hardly anyone, but still, on the weekend I probably hear three four-wheel-drives go by. I once saw a dirt-bike rider in full leathers and a helmet driving over the sandstone hills.

In the last two days, I've found some great things in the desert. One was a porcupine quill as long as a pen and as sharp as a dart. It is really an amazing piece of defensive equipment. But in fact, it isn't meant to be only a defensive measure like a wall around a city or an armadillo that rolls up in a ball to protect itself. No, the porcupine is much different. It doesn't just protect with its quills; it inflicts major damage to any attacker with those quills.

But the real find was an ibex horn! It's crescent shaped, hollow, gray in color, has at least ten bumps on it (which means it's ten years old), and is as long as from my elbow to the end of my fingertips. Tamir will be jealous! Last night I walked to a part of the desert I hadn't been to before (duh! I haven't been to most of the desert). It was getting dark, the mosquitoes were coming out, and as I walked quickly back through a riverbed, I almost passed by the ibex horn because it looked like an old tire tread. When I looked closer, I couldn't believe my eyes—an ibex horn! I filled it with water in order to kill any bugs or scorpions that might live inside. I wonder if Israeli and U.S. customs will care when I take it back home.

For most of my stay here, the song "Wonderful World" has kept playing in my head. I can hear Louis Armstrong sing about life's wonder, love, and beauty. And his voice! You can hear in his voice that he lived the words he sang. All the more impressive that he grew up a black man in a racist society. How do some people do it? Become "love filled" in a society that's often unloving . . .

Anyway, I guess I'm singing that song to myself because *I feel that way too*. As screwed up as life is, it—and the people in it—can be pretty incredible and wonderful.

"Ohhhh yeah!"

I walked into a "standoff." Near my cave there was a gecko two feet away from a dark-eyed brown mouse. Their eyes were locked on each other.

"Go on, mouse," said the gecko, "make your move."

"No," the mouse said, "you make the first move."

But I interrupted all that. They stared each other down while I stood there, then the mouse looked over at me and then back at the gecko and then back at me, as if to say, "Okay, gecko, the marshal here saved your life. But we'll meet again, and when we do, he won't be there to help you."

The mouse eyeballed me one more time before turning away and getting on his horse. The gecko's eyes never left the mouse, even after the mouse had disappeared over a stone ridge.

day 31

Yesterday I happened to glance over at a bush and saw a multicolored miniature bamboo lantern. It was two inches long, made out of small stalks, and hanging from a tree. I figured it was a toy or a locket carried here by the winter floods.

I pulled it from the tree, and upon closer inspection, I yelled out, "No way! There is no freakin' way!"

A little caterpillar was living in it. When I looked back at the bush, I saw that there were other tiny lanterns, all with little caterpillars living in them. The caterpillars clung to the branches with their front legs while holding on to the lantern house from within with their back legs. The house was made with stalks of various sizes, each between one-quarter and one-half inch long, fitted together perfectly—so perfectly that it was beyond my comprehension or belief that a caterpillar could actually cut the sticks so precisely and then glue the corners together.

"No way!" I shouted again. "There is no way a caterpillar made that!"

But there it was—right in front of my face—the fact was the

caterpillars made these small lanterns/cocoons, and still my mind refused to believe it.

I woke up in my tent this morning with fifteen to twenty ants running off with my food. I didn't know how they got in. They didn't seem to know either. They ran around in circles trying to get out. I had to eliminate them. I didn't want to, and I thought of setting them all free, but then wouldn't they come back for more food and bring friends? While walking around the desert, I've seen armies of ants with thousands to a group. I don't want to wake up with a thousand ants crawling on me and throughout my tent.

I woke up to the sound of growling during the night. I also heard something ripping into my garbage bags. Perhaps one of the two or three leopards left in the Judean desert? Maybe a wolf? Or what about a hyena? They're especially nasty looking. I bet they laugh only when they're eating you. Then I heard more growling. I remained still and attentive until I heard it a third time and realized it was coming from my own stomach. It must have been all that pasty pasta I ate last night. I sure hope Tamir and Ya'el get here with my tuna soon.

In prayer/meditation, I cried again today. As I cried, I remembered the dream of stroking my sick and dying mother's head. My breathing was labored, like it was when climbing down the cliff. Somehow my breathing and my fear and grief were all connected.

I cried and felt the intense pain of losing someone I loved. The pain seemed unbearable, the kind of pain that makes you ask God, "Why? What did I do wrong to deserve this pain?"

"You didn't do anything wrong," God said.

"Then why? Why?" I sobbed.

"Because you loved her—and you love people."

"But why?" I asked. "Why did you make us so that we love things that die? And why did you make those things, those people, so that they would die?"

My final questions were met with silence—the kind of silence that told me the answer could never be found in words.

What's called guru yoga in Tibetan Buddhism is similar to having a relationship with Jesus. In guru yoga, a student develops a close relationship to the lama, or spiritual teacher. Since the spiritual teacher is (in theory) more open to God's presence than the student, the student can access that presence by being open to the teacher. The presence of God is palpable in the teacher. This is what Jesus meant when he said, "I am the way to the Father" (see John 14:6). If you believe Jesus's death took away your sins, then you let go of the sins and the guilt. And if you experience his love, that dissolves any self-judgment and fear. Then you're able to sink into this presence and experience it.

Ever since I first heard the word *Dzogchen* twenty years ago, I've been drawn to its teaching. It is among the highest meditation practices in all of Tibetan Buddhism, but I never could find anyone who taught it. One lama even told me that "Dzogchen isn't for children," which is ironic, because Jesus said, "Bring to me the children" (see Mark 10:14), and when I was later taught Dzogchen by Chokyi Nyima, I immediately thought of Jesus.

Dzogchen introduces you (if you are ready) to your true nature. And that's what Jesus does. Even now, if I am feeling lost, I will sometimes think of Jesus, and then I see and experience his being in me. He then says, "Look at me," and I look so completely, and surrender so completely, that I see where I am resisting his love; and then my resistance releases and there is only Christ. Nothing is outside of this Being, so supreme is it— and that is what Dzogchen teaches.

Dzogchen also aims at overcoming the same narrow and egocentric view that Jesus helps people transform. This preoccupation with fear and self-judgment (the Buddhists believe) takes away a human being's ability to experience the panoramic view of Spirit or Supreme Being.

Now that my forty days are down to ten, I find myself looking toward the end but still trying to pull myself back to *now*. I notice my energy, my excitement—even my distractions—are increasing. Something in me knows I can waste my time, distract myself from the present for a few days, and I'll almost be out of here. Done.

But rappelling those cliffs keeps coming back to me. I was so scared and uncomfortable then that I wanted it over so that I could go back to my old life, my cave, and things that I knew— things that were comfortable and did not demand I look too deeply or be with myself too deeply. If I ever go rappelling again,

I *will* pay more attention. I won't be thinking about the end as much while still in the middle, or even when close to the end.

I once knew a man who did everything only once. When I asked him why, he said, "It's because everything I do, I do completely."

We have to respect God and Jesus. *Respect* comes from the Latin, meaning "to look again." We have to constantly look at God and at Jesus to see how our understanding of them has changed. Don't depend on the understanding of God you found forty years ago, or twenty, or five, or one year ago, or even a moment ago. Each moment, look again at God and respect God. Love is an understanding that happens now—not yesterday.

> *I can never escape from your spirit!*
>   *I can never get away from your presence!*
> *If I go up to heaven, you are there;*
>   *if I go down to the place of the dead, you are there.*
>   —Psalm 139:7–8 NLT

Often in my prayer and meditation sessions, I feel the movement of energies, then a physical tensing or resisting, then fear, then I often cry some, then a release, then an awareness of the energy of Being or Spirit. This cycle will frequently repeat itself. But this time while I was crying and seeing it, the crying seemed to shift, and then I realized that *crying is also Being.*

And then I had the subtle realization that I previously "hid" in crying. But now that crying "saw"; that crying was Being, and I couldn't hide in it. Then I went to fear, and I realized that fear was Being also. That every speck of fear "saw" truly.

Then I went to my bodily tensions and contractions—but I couldn't hide there either. Everywhere I tried to hide was Being and had "eyes"—*it saw*. And this went faster and faster until there was nowhere I could hide from Being or from myself. Then I thought of calling one of my spiritual teachers about this, but I couldn't even hide in that thought. Finally, it all became horrible, overwhelming, and totally crazy because I couldn't hide anywhere, and everyplace was nakedly seen—and seeing. I cried at the horror of not being able to hide, the horrible seeing of it all. Like a man yearning for a dark place to sleep, but even the dark is light to him! I felt the insanity of nowhere to hide; then I laughed, and even my laughter was seen through and was "seeing" itself.

I saw myself and everyplace I hid with a naked, diamond-clear, and razor-sharp awareness that destroyed me and sliced me down to nothing—and yet the all-pervading love of God was indivisible and present throughout the experience. I found myself feeling shame and saying "I'm sorry" several times, but it was always preempted by God's love. There was not a flicker, a blank spot, or a hesitation in the love of God's Being. There was no judgment at all, no comments at all—only love.

"I am the Alpha and Omega," Jesus said (Revelation 22:13). The words *Alpha* and *Omega* are Greek for "first" and "last,"

"beginning" and "end." Jesus went to the desert in order to consummate his love for the Beloved, in order for his yearning to commune with that which he yearned for. Jesus was the beginning; God, the Supreme Being, was his end. In the desert, Jesus reconciled the tension between human and Being and was astounded to find that he, the holiest of men, was a human Being.

If I close my eyes and imagine love, there are no edges and no end to it. Jesus is love. Thus, there is no end to him.

Jesus said, "Believe in the Light, so that you may become sons of Light" (John 12:36 NASB).

Jesus was saying he is Light, and if you "believe" by aligning with him, you align with the Light.

Humanity's potential will be realized when the "Son of Man" is who *we* are. God made us in his "image"—an image that is still being developed. Developed by God, so that one day we will become a beautiful picture of what it means to be a "son of man" or "human being." On that day, Jesus's words "The Son of Man must be lifted up" (John 3:14) will come true.

When Tamir first showed me the desert thirty-three days ago, I remember our car passing a dark-skinned man driving a tractor. The man slowed down while making a turn and looked back at his trailer, which was piled high with boxes of green peppers. He looked very concerned. Then his cart went slowly over a crack in the road—*that was it*. He was worried that his boxes of peppers, stacked six crates high, would come tumbling down. There was a story there, a time when everything had come tumbling down—and it all was written on that man's face.

I dreamed of John Smith, the only person in my grade school who was close to me in grade-point achievements. Before my parents got sick and died, I loved learning, and I was beating him grade-point-wise (excuse me for thinking that way in fifth grade). But after they died I lost interest and wound up as a B–C student throughout high school, while he got scholarships. In the dream, he was telling me how I was kicking his tail in grade school. He was so genuinely noncompetitive about the past, while lavishing me with compliments, that I began to like him and I thought of us as friends.

I guess he represented what I could have been if things had gone differently. I've thought about that from time to time as I've struggled to pay bills, lived in a mobile home, and had little drive to achieve academically or financially.

It's amazing to me how many things we grieve—or fail to grieve. I wouldn't want to be anyone other than who I am now. I wouldn't want another person's life. Still, I'm sad for the life never lived, or perhaps it's the loss of innocence. The kind of innocence that a person has early in life, when they think if they just do well in school, get a good job, and make money, then everything will be okay. But when people around you start dying, that innocence is shattered, and everything changes.

It's my birthday today. I am forty-two years old. I called Tamir and Ya'el yesterday to tell them I was running low on food. I ordered ten cans of tuna, two packages of whole-wheat pita bread, and some granola. Since it was my birthday, I also asked for a watermelon.

"Ya'el is going to be at the hostel tomorrow," Tamir said. "So she will bring it."

It's 3:00 p.m. on my birthday. I walked to the hostel to pick up the food. There wasn't any. So I called Ya'el.

"I am in Jerusalem with my kids. I will bring the food by tonight," she said.

When you've been in the desert for thirty-two days, you can't help but look forward to a can of tuna and a watermelon. So while I waited for Ya'el, every hour seemed like forever, especially because I hadn't eaten much the last few days. Yesterday I had two cups of powdered soy milk and my last two Clif Bars. Today I ate nothing, figuring I'd just wait for some decent food. But when my treats didn't get here, I ate what I had lying around—some old white pita bread and olive oil. Put a little salt on it and add a cup of coffee—it was a special birthday meal! Hooray! As I ate my feast, I sang, "They say it's your birthday! Dada-dada-dada—it's my birthday too!"

Halfway through the first piece of bread, I saw a big glob of mold on it. I tossed that piece away and inspected the next piece. It looked fine. As I dipped it in olive oil and finished it, I couldn't help but wonder why there was this big glob of green mold on the other piece. I glanced at the almost-empty bottle of olive oil that I had been dipping into, and *yuck*! It had little green and brown floaters in there. They looked like furry mushrooms.

I put everything down, even my disgust at what I had been eating. I picked up my cup of freeze-dried coffee and leaned back against the cave wall. The sky was clear blue. The cliffs, brown and ash colored. A smile came to my lips. There was beauty all around me, and together with a cup of nasty, sugar-laden coffee, it was a perfect moment and a perfect birthday treat.

Each day since I got rid of the bees, more and more geckos come back. They are territorial, and when they "cluck," sometimes they're answered by a gecko halfway across the canyon, while at other times, it's a warning to a nearby gecko to "beat it." The odd thing is that when they fight, the retreating gecko rarely runs very far away. He's always just a few feet in front of the aggressor, which leads to what I think is an unnecessary chase and stop, chase and stop, chase and stop, all along the rock face. One time, just before disappearing behind a rock ledge, the gecko being chased stuck his tail up in the air as though giving his pursuer the finger, wiggling it around while making all sorts of hissing and cackling noises. Come to think of it, maybe they're not fighting—maybe it's a mating ritual? The beginning of a fight and the beginning of love both involve an intimate dance of some sort.

The tuxedo bird is back, chasing mice from under a low-hanging rock face next to my cave. Two weeks ago, the same bird chased away two mice, and then a week after that a mouse chased out a snake—and now the tuxedo bird is back chasing out the mice again. I saw their two tiny rear ends scampering over a small, rocky ridge as the sharp-beaked and sharp-dressed bird ran a few steps after them.

Who really lives there anyway? I wondered—like some nosy neighbor who peeks through her curtains, watching various people come and go at the house next door.

I threw a piece of white pita bread about ten feet from where I pray. Only one bird has been tempted to eat it so far. He was a needle-beaked black bird. After he landed, he hopped around but didn't go for the bread right away. He was smart. His strategy consisted of looking in every direction and every possible predator's hiding place—and screeching the most god-awful screech you have ever heard. Sort of like the sound of fingernails running down a blackboard with the volume pumped up. It made you want to shout, "Stop it!" and "Shut up!" That was the bird's strategy, to get on a lurking predator's nerves so much that he blurted out, "Shut up!" and blew his cover. Eventually the bird pecked at the white flour pita and decided it wasn't worth eating.

The screeching bird returned twenty minutes later with a friend. The friend sat high up on the stone ledge and watched while the other bird flew over to the bread. The whole time there was constant communication, but it wasn't an ugly-sounding screech; instead, it was a high-pitched, lilting, "everything's fine" sound. The bird on the ground felt so much safer because the other bird was looking out for it. Occasionally the bird on the ground made a sweet sound, too, as if to say, "You still watching?" Then his high-vantage-point friend would answer, "Everything's fine."

They still didn't take the bread, though.

The screeching bird never did get its bread. The bread was dry, and every time the bird pecked at it, it made a sound the bird wasn't expecting, and so the bird got scared and flew away. We can be like that in that sometimes the Spirit appears in a form that scares us, and instead of going toward God, we run from God.

"No way," Eli, the rappelling instructor, said to me after I asked him if it was easy for him and his friends to talk with their girlfriends or wives about their feelings and emotions.

"No way," he repeated. "We call it Israeli macho—most of us were in the army or Special Forces, and after doing that, it's hard to talk about feelings."

"It was hard for me to learn," I said. "I come from a family of Chicago cops."

"That's worse than the military!" Eli said.

Talking about feelings is the same as rappelling a cliff face. Actually, they shouldn't call it rappelling, because although you're rappelling or pushing away from the face of the cliff, you're actually "inviting" yourself into the present. You're inviting your fear, your resistance, your skill, your ability to adapt and grow, your joy, your love, your excitement—everything you are—even your soul is being invited into the present moment. Talking to those you love about your feelings is no different from rappelling the cliff face or "inviting." You bring everything you are to it. One man fears rappelling a cliff—another fears rappelling his feelings. Actually, the refusal to rappel or invite your feelings has killed or taken many more lives than rappelling a cliff face. Because life happens each moment, and each moment you refuse to rappel or go over that edge is a way of killing your life, one moment at a time.

That's why I came to the desert—to rappel each moment; to invite each moment of my soul. Because if a human being can stay in one spot and invite the fearful edges close, if he can go past those edges and rappel through his soul and through his Being, then he can go anywhere in the world, inside and out, and be free to face the moment whether it's in the face of a cliff, the face of a lover, or even the face of God.

When I rappelled that cliff, my fear narrowed my soul's presence until all I saw was fear. I was small and closed. But as I continued, I began to open and enjoy. Each moment of our lives gives us the choice, the opportunity, either to be fearful, small, and closed, or to open and enjoy.

By the time I had climbed down the third cliff, I was enjoying it. The only difference between the first cliff face and the last was me.

When I told Eli about the big armored-looking fly that bit me, he said, "That sounds like a Jericho fly. They lay eggs in your bloodstream. You may want to get checked."

It's my birthday, and Ya'el won't be at the hostel till after 9:00 p.m. with my food—and *my birthday watermelon*.

"Tomorrow she can bring it," Tamir said.

"No way," I said. "It's my birthday—and I want to celebrate! I want my watermelon. I'll walk in tonight and get it."

day 33

I walked the three miles to the hostel in the dark last night. I kept to the gravel road, which is a longer route, because there was less chance of stepping on a snake. I wore a long-sleeved shirt and long pants, together with my mosquito net hat, in case the wind died and the mosquitoes attacked.

After I got to Ya'el's apartment, she called and said it would be another one to two hours before she arrived. I lay down on a couch in the dark. Her single room at the hostel was the last room in the last building, and right next to the desert. Actually, the whole complex was in the desert and attracted either tourists or people who were trying to figure out what to do next in their lives. People like Ya'el, who was fresh from a divorce and a drastic change of religion; or Kate the Brit, who had warned me about scorpions the first day I arrived and who later told me her heart was broken.

"The reason why you're having a tough time," I told her, "is because you're a kind and sensitive person."

She looked at me with tears in her eyes, and then she touched her heart as a way of saying, "Thank you." As I walked away, she called out to me and said, "But why is it that kind and sensitive people are always the ones to get dumped on?"

I didn't answer her because she didn't want an answer, and that's why she was at the hostel. It was the last outpost; the final attempt by civilization to control the wilderness that lay beyond.

I opened the windows in Ya'el's room, but even then, as I lay on the couch, the room felt dead. There were no sounds of nature: no buzzing, no birdcalls, no wind. This life among inanimate objects was sterile, and even the air and the energy felt stagnant—not vibrant or alive. I had never felt like this before, as though the outdoors were more my home than indoors.

I'm going to miss my desert, I realized sadly. *I'm going to miss my family when I leave!* The bees, the flies, and even my pain-in-the-neck relatives, the mosquitoes. The birds—all those unique-sounding birds! The beautiful ibex coming to my canyon to feed. My cave—with her stony face carved out by millions of years of winter rain. And the sky—the open sky! I could never begin to fill its space with my puny mind and thoughts. And, of course, the rocks: big, small, sharp, and smooth. Some I step on, some I climb over, and others I just go around. They all feel like family, and as these weeks have passed, I've resisted them less until they are no longer outside but inside me. They are another part of my being, living with, alongside, and among my thoughts, emotions, and body. The other day while praying/meditating, I heard a bee buzz nearby and I was startled because I thought he was going to fly through me! Through the debris I call "me"—those thoughts, emotions, memories that seem to move and exist in the same Supreme Being that the bee moves in. Suddenly the home I was going to didn't seem as much like home.

"You ate some," Ya'el said after opening up her refrigerator.

"I couldn't help it," I replied. She was talking about an unopened bag of chocolate-dipped cookies that had been in her freezer. While I waited for her to arrive, I had peeked in her freezer and saw a bag that had Hebrew writing on it, and pictures of chocolate-dipped cookies. What was I supposed to do? *It was meant to be.* Just like that day the six cliff rappellers showed up. It was unavoidable destiny and Divine plan. I ate half the bag.

"Here," she said, tossing me the rest of the cookies. "Happy Birthday."

I'm a grown man. I'm forty-two years old, and my mother died thirty years ago! Thirty years!

So why am I crying for her like a baby? Why am I still grieving her death?

I cried a lot in my last prayer and meditation time. I was even ready to quit early because I couldn't stand it. That's when I prayed to God and Jesus for help.

"Where do you feel the pain?" Jesus asked, which was good because it helped me to focus on where in my body-mind-psyche the pain was, rather than just complaining about some general all-over-the-place kind of pain.

I found the pain in my chest, not the kind of pain from getting shot or stabbed, but the kind of pain from being deeply hurt. I started to cry, then sob, and then I prayed again to "be delivered." I saw myself as that twelve-year-old boy sitting on the floor watching TV as his mother rubbed his head, which had been one of the safest, most secure, and most loving experiences of my life. What more could I want? I had a television, and I had my mother's love and head rubbing! And I was still oblivious to the inevitable pain that life could and would inflict.

As I cried, I heard myself say, "I want it to be how it used to be. I want my mom back." As unrealistic as the adult "me" knew that was, someone in me still wished it. I wept for a while, and then I was the twelve-year-old boy back in my sister's basement after my mom died. Alone. In the dark of my basement bedroom, wishing and praying that somehow someone would come for me, that someone would save me from the overwhelming, unspeakable confusion and pain.

"But no one came for me," I cried again. "They just left me down there."

I found myself wanting to be done with crying and with my grief, much like I wanted the rappelling done after the first cliff. But what could I do? After thirty years, someone or something in me felt safe enough to grieve. The crying continued.

After I stopped, I climbed out of my cave and ascended the twenty or so feet to the plateau. I walked to my tent, got the watermelon, cut it in half, and stood on the plateau—eating watermelon as the sun went down.

"You know," I said out loud, "a chair would be nice about now.

"Anybody got a chair?" I shouted.

The desert color was especially bright and beautiful after having cried my eyes clear. I was suddenly aware that I was pretty happy.

"Hey, Dave," I shouted. "You're missing the party!" Then I walked over to a rock and sat down. When I was done with the watermelon, I left it out on the plateau. I was sure someone would eat the rest. I stood up, with the blade of my pocketknife still out, and pointed it up at the sky.

"C'mon, big guy," I said as I moved around like a guy in a knife fight—dodging this way and that. "Let's see what you got!"

I stopped after a few moments with a big smile on my face and went back to my tent. I made a cup of powdered soy milk and ate the rest of the chocolate-dipped cookies. It was the closest I've come to "pigging out" since I've been here. Happy Birthday to me!

day 34

I woke up very groggy and heavy feeling. My thoughts were slow and clunky, as though I had to collect rocks and make large letters on the desert plateau, spelling out "Get up" or "Move."

As soon as I got to my cave, I fell into a three-hour deep sleep. Many images came and went. In one of them I was standing at the edge of the cliff, feeling my fear as I backed over the edge. Then I jumped into the abyss, and I was totally my fear. No longer separated from it, I was my fear completely. As I was falling, the fear I had felt standing at the edge and the tension around it disappeared. I relaxed into the falling, and I felt like eternity itself. I woke up remembering a poem, "The Falling," which I had written many years earlier.

> *My heart is falling through itself*
> *farther than I could have imagined.*
>
> *Past my fears,*
> *my wants,*

and even
my loves.

It falls into itself
in order to be renewed,
a pit without bottom.

I realize now
that my whole life has been a falling,
a continual falling.

To live in a body
with feet firmly placed
and a heart that is eternally falling.

I ask, "How?"

How can I live this way?

You say, "Like me."

In my frustration
I reply that
"the likes of you
has no stomach for falling.
So do not lecture me!"

My kindred spirit is a waterfall.
It gushes as it weeps,

yet descends in exuberance
at its falling.

Show me a way
to live
with this falling,
and I will show you
the way of those before me.

In the waters remains the mystery.

Quietude.
Sadness.
Pain.
Life.
It is there.

My fountain has rained
and the earth is renewed.
It is alive again.

My life is always in motion.
It is always falling,
and yet
I walk upon this earth.

A small flying bug, who rapidly flaps its wings like a humming-bird, often stops outside my mosquito net and investigates me.

I've been tossing the pair of screeching birds some bread. One will grab a piece and fly away, saying, "I got it." And his friend will follow, saying, "You got it?"

"I got it!"

"You sure?"

"I'm sure!"

"All right!"

Today's been incredibly hot. Yesterday was hot also. What's hot? Hot is when I sit in my cave naked, not moving—yet I still sweat like crazy. It's so hot that after only two minutes of lying on my side, the insides of my thighs are soaking wet from one lying on the other. It's so hot that it's very quiet; neither bug nor bird nor animal wants to exert itself.

6:30 P.M.

I went for a walk through the wadi where I found the ibex horn. I passed various rocks: black, gray, white, red, brown, and a mix of some or all of those colors. Every single rock is on its way to becoming sand. At the end of the wadi was a kind of stage made of stone: eight feet high, thirty feet long, and thirty feet deep. When I looked closer at this rock, I was amazed to find it was mainly composed of seashells and stones embedded in the rock. It must be millions of years old and is made of millions of formerly alive sea creatures. Compared to the age of that rock, my life is not even a blip on the radar screen of time.

As I walked back through the wadi tonight, I thought about going home.

Then I can relax! I thought.

"Relax?" I asked myself. "Why don't you relax here?

"At home I can relax," I said.

"Relax what?" I asked, remembering all the letting go of tension I had done through meditation and prayer.

"Here," I said, putting my hand near my upper chest. "I'm holding here.

"Relax it," I suggested.

"I can't," I said. "It's the only thing left I have to hold on to.

"Whether you 'hold or don't hold,'" I said, "it doesn't matter; you're still Being—still in God's presence."

Suddenly I stopped identifying my essence or soul with "holding" and relaxed into Being. My "holding" stood naked, alone in the midst of Being. I started to cry in the middle of the dry desert riverbed. I knew I could tell myself to let go even more into God, but I sensed that it wasn't time to push too hard. I was a human being, and my goal was not to push myself into becoming some kind of pure spirit overnight, but to let the spirit unfold in its time, not mine.

Sometimes I have this bad habit of thinking something bad is going to happen when I'm feeling too good or if I'm "playing" too much. It must be a leftover reaction from loving people— which makes me happy—and then having them die.

day 35

Last night a critter kept messing with the tarp outside my tent. The crinkling sound it made kept me awake. I yelled a few times because this scares away mice, but it made no difference. Finally, I discovered the culprit.

A black beetle. I had put a tarp under my tent and one on the floor inside the tent. I figured if a scorpion or a snake decided to live under my tent, and then one night tried to bite or sting me through the floor, three layers of plastic would be hard to get through. The black beetle was walking on the outside tarp, and that tarp is very stiff and crackly. So whenever he walked on it, it sounded like someone walking on potato chips. I didn't bother him though; I just let him do his King Kong imitation.

The end of my forty days is nearing. I wonder if Jesus thought about that. If he thought, *Moses was on the mountain with God for forty days, so I'll stay exactly forty days too—that means I have five days left!*

I am increasingly aware of my wanting it to be over, wanting to go home. So that has become part of my prayer and meditation.

What is it, I wonder, *that is resisting the Now by thinking and looking ahead to the future?*

Jesus said that only the alive can see the alive. Aliveness is the fire of the soul, and its only fuel is Now. Live anywhere but Now, and the soul fire goes out and we become like the "whitewashed tombs" Jesus spoke about—beautiful on the outside but filled with bones and rotting corpses on the inside (see Matthew 23:27).

It's hard surrendering to the present or the Presence because you have to see the stuff that you're surrendering; things such as the pain, the fears, the demons, the hurts, and the plain ignorance—which drove us into a dead end in our lives—are seen as we turn around and walk past them on the way out. That's why I'm looking toward the end of these forty days. *I don't want to see anymore; I don't want to feel anymore.* I've seen enough! I spent my forty-two years of life building a place within myself that shielded me from what I didn't want to know; and these last thirty-five days, I've found myself reliving my forty-two years and finding pieces of my soul hidden here and there—in places I neither knew of nor wanted to enter.

I've been throwing bread to the screeching birds. They don't really screech anymore. I guess they realized sweet sounds will get them everything. They are now coming to within a few feet of me. I tried to get one to take bread from my hand, but I guess it's still too early yet. When they come looking for food and I'm napping, they come close and talk bird talk to me.

"Hey, buddy," they say. "Got any more of that bread?"

Now that they come closer, I can see they are all black except for an orange stripe on each wing.

Meanwhile, a mouse tried to sneak up on me while I was meditating. But I heard him coming. He was very clumsy, kicking over small pebbles and bumping right into my roll of duct tape.

"Hey!" I yelled. "Get out of here!"

Then I clapped my hands loudly. He scampered away, but I didn't see him come out from under the stone crevice behind me. I heard him a minute later, and turning to my left, I saw him looking right at me with big brown eyes.

"Beat it!" I shouted as he turned and ran down the cliff. "If you think looking at me with those big brown eyes is going to work, think again!

"That barely works with a woman!" I said. "So it certainly isn't going to work coming from a pudgy, hairy rodent!"

Just then I heard a sound to my right.

"And you," I said, turning to my right and seeing a mouse who was now scurrying under the low-hanging rock face three feet away. "I'm talking to you too! And you'd better talk to your friend about coming over here!"

I've only got a few days left in this desert, so I'm trying to maintain some order.

I gave myself another two-pitcher shower, and then I sang a song by the Doors while dancing in the moonlight and conducting an imaginary orchestra.

"C'mon and touch me, babe . . . Da-Danau—can't you see that I am not afraid! Da-Danau—what was that promise that you made . . ."

Then I looked up and saw the reddest planet I've ever seen.

"You sure are red!" I shouted at the top of my lungs. "Red! Red! Red!"

Then I went to sleep—*feeling very still.*

day 36

The two black-and-orange birds come five times a day now. If I'm meditating, they talk to me, looking for food.

"We're here," they say. When I don't move, they speak again.

"In case you didn't know," they say again, "we're here!"

And five minutes later they say, "We're just waiting for you; don't mind us . . ." They come within three or four feet, but that seems to be their limit. I usually feed them bread, some apple cores too. They will tap the bread on the ground a few times, and if it's too hard, they won't take it.

The bottom of my spine is hurting more and more. It's very hard to sit; one moment it's powerful energy moving, and the next moment it's very painful. What am I doing here, anyway? Why does it have to be hard work and painful? Am I making it harder than it has to be? Am I doing something wrong?

Why can't I just say, "Okay, God, I'm ready. I've got ten minutes to kill, so make me and shape me so that I'm 100 percent of the time experiencing the bliss of your presence."

And then it's done!

Why couldn't God have given us a better way? He could have put the Tree of the Knowledge of Good and Evil up on the moon, instead of in the middle of the Garden, and we wouldn't have found it till 1969.

Some things are beyond my understanding.

I've had it. I'm kind of angry at this whole thing. Maybe my tantrum ten days ago needs a repeat.

I decided to make myself a cup of coffee. A very small cup. I usually have a small cup every third day. I'm trying to limit myself because I don't want to be propped up by caffeine while I'm here. I want to see what "I am."

But I had another cup today even though I had one yesterday. So it's crazy that I'm second-guessing myself over a small cup of instant coffee. Right? C'mon, really; I need your input now, because this is my thirty-sixth day, and I don't think I can tell "crazy" from "not crazy" anymore.

While I'm getting my coffee, a fly keeps landing on my face.

"Fly," I said, "you don't want to mess with me today. I'm not in the mood."

Lucky for him he disappeared at that point; I was ready to flatten him.

Ya'el stopped by with my last supply of water. We talked about Being and boundaries, and how our Being often seeks to be defined by its surroundings.

"You have to put something soft in the corners of a crib," she said, "because a baby always goes to the corner when it sleeps. It wants to feel something against its head. Same thing with clothes; up till about three months old, a baby will cry when you take off its clothes. It doesn't like to be naked, and clothes give a feeling of boundary to a baby."

"Like Adam and Eve," she continued. "They tried to hide from God because they were naked."

I have just about four days left. I could goof off for four days and be done! But I want to open even more at the end, not close off or distract myself. Maybe the ultimate in faith is just to let the last four days be what they are. Oh boy, I feel another philosophical debate coming on; how much do you allow the moment to "be" versus how much do you add to the moment and manipulate it?

I guess that's why people wanted ten commandments. It takes away the guesswork. But then people used laws and commandments to control the Spirit of God. They wanted a God whose movements and actions they could anticipate. A scientific spirituality that says, "If I do this, then God will react that way."

Each moment became a logical and mathematical problem to work out.

"Let's see: this circumstance + that person = this command-ment. I have the answer to this moment. It's written here on page such-and-such."

It seems to me that God has been asking me to be two things since the day I was born. First, to be a good and just human being; and second, to be a fool for my heart's desires.

A good human being would never go to the desert for forty days; only a fool would go and, in so doing, find his heart's desire.

day 37

Being here is very strange: one moment I'm weeping; the next I'm happy. One moment I'm suffering some unnamable deep pain while cursing God and the universe for it, and the next moment I'm glad to be relieved of it and to be alive. One moment I'm sad about leaving; the next I can't wait to get home. And one moment my butt hurts—and the next moment it still hurts.

I threw my two bird friends a big piece of bread. So big, they couldn't carry it and instead ate as much as they could and then flew away. It was cute watching them, because as each one ate, the other one stood guard. Every once in a while, the one watching said in bird language, "I'm looking around, and everything is fine." Reminds me of the old Hindu saying: "Two birds sit in a tree. One eats of the fruit while the other watches." I've also seen them regurgitate pits and different-colored berries. They must eat everything they find and just count on keeping half of it down.

That's why I came to the desert: "only eating" from the tree wasn't good enough. It's an empty, self-serving existence that has too much "is this all there is?" to it. When you are just one bird eating, you're scared as you eat, because you also have to watch out for being eaten. But if you discover the part of you that always sees, then you are saved even if you die, because seeing fully—in the way that Jesus saw, in the way that God sees, in the way that we do see but fail to recognize—is eternal life and Supreme Being. It's a seeing that comes straight from the eyes of God, into and through our eyes and into this world.

Sometimes I cry, and I feel that I'm torturing myself for no reason, that it shouldn't be this painful. When I ask God if I'm doing anything wrong or what I can do differently, all I get is the same reply over and over. It's the look of love and the words "We love you."

Sometimes I will ask Jesus for help, and he will just tell me to look at him in the way that, looking totally—100 percent—I become what I look at. Then I often feel that who I have been or think I am is framed by love, allowing "this bundle of knotted me" to let go into the surrounding love and Being.

That's why I'm so afraid of death lately. I'm opening to Being and the reality of the fleeting existence of my life—of all people's lives. I am voluntarily letting go into this experience, but still I'm kicking and screaming as I go. That's why I went to the desert—because people can't hear you kicking and screaming as you die the spiritual death in the desert. Back in the city, there are too many people who love me, who would try to pull me back (out of love) to a life I'm freely giving up. That's why Jesus called Peter "Satan." Peter loved Jesus and tried to pull Jesus back into the life Peter wanted for Jesus, and not the life the Spirit wanted for Jesus.

I know I'm not Jesus—well, in some deep ways we all are— but what he went through, I go through, and we all go through. To see how he did it, to see how he lived this amazing, incredible, horrible existence we call being "a human being," gives me so much courage to go on; but it's not simply courage. It's something much more. Through Jesus I'm being given "a connection to Being" that has already accomplished what I'm attempting to do. When one human being accomplishes something, it is embedded into the soul of all, so that each human being has access to that experience. By touching that experience, it becomes our experience—exploding and unfolding uniquely into our lives. Jesus said, "You are in me, and I am in you" (John 14:20).

It was true two thousand years ago, and it is true now.

day 38

I dreamed of an older Chinese man who, during a break at work, went outside and looked through a barbed-wire fence at a tree. Then the trees started to bud and bloom. He was filled with understanding, enlightenment, and joy. He was so absorbed by what he saw that he stayed there, staring, for I don't know how long. When he turned to walk away, part of his mustache and lip tore off on the barbed fence because he had been there so long that his lip and mustache had grown around the fence.

He went back to his work very happy. He continued to have deep experiences, and as he had those experiences in the dream, I could feel myself in my actual body sleeping in my bed having the same realizations. I was aware of crying and the Spirit moving in my body while I slept.

In my prayer and meditation, I've realized that when I am noticing states of mind like "tensing" or "pressure" or "holding" or "unpleasantness," it's both unnecessary and unwise to wait for or expect these states of mind to change. The purpose of noticing them is to see that they are occurring within my Being and are not solely who I am; rather, these states of mind are something happening within who I am. I am not as "stuck" in "feeling stuck" or in needing these mind states to change. Increasingly, I sense and identify more with the Beingness in which it all takes place.

Jesus told the story about the thief who breaks in, but the owner of the house sees him—so the thief takes nothing. If the Being or soul sees what the mind is doing, the mind will not be able to hijack or hypnotize the soul; thus, it will not be able to steal away the eternal life and love that is and has always been a part of the Being.

I've got new motivations, new goals and rewards. The first is that I allow myself a half cup of coffee after my third session of prayer and meditation.

The second is that I try to be done with my prayer and meditation sessions by 6:30 p.m. Then I can go for a one-hour walk and take a two-pitcher shower when I get back.

Tamir stopped by after dark with his roommate, Mikael, and Mikael's girlfriend, (also named) Ya'el. It was very nice talking with someone in the desert on a windy night. Tamir brought some cereal for my breakfast the last three days. This made me incredibly happy to have good meals to look forward to. Also, Mikael is the new cook at the hostel. So in seventy-two hours when I leave here, I will go to the hostel and Mikael will make apple strudel with ice cream for me! That's the last time I will mention it or think about it, because already my mouth is watering. And if I've learned anything here in the desert, it's this: When you are eating apple strudel, time goes by quickly. When you are waiting for apple strudel, it goes by slowly.

My meditation and prayer sessions are often painful. It's more on a psychic, soul, and spirit level—and its echo is located physically in my chest. Sometimes I cry so much, and even then I feel I'm still holding back. So today I looked at Jesus and God again, and I wished they could save me from this. Instead, they looked at me with love, and I relaxed into that love and cried harder.

Why I cry in prayer:

1. Releasing of soul tension, which comes from being a human being.

2. Grieving my parents' deaths, my friends' deaths, and my death—and all the deaths and losses to come.

3. When fear is seen and released, often it is through tears.

4. The dying of the old me and the birth of the new.

5. Who knows why I cry? I just let it happen and trust that it needs to happen—that's called faith.

Some habits are so ingrained. For example, every once in a while when I climb out of my cave and up to the plateau, I check to see if I have my house keys while I am walking to my tent so that I can let myself in.

Other times, I climb out of my cave and say to myself, "Let's see if I got any mail."

I feel like I'm on *The Flintstones*. I was taking a walk, and I thought of a few things I didn't want to forget. Since I didn't have my notebook, I picked up a flat stone and scratched notes on it with another stone.

As I walked down to the edge, it amazed me how everything is a part of keeping me mindful and keeping my heart focused on being here spiritually, which of course means just being here fully as a human being. I can't stray too far from prayer. After my prayer/meditation session is up, what can I do to get away from the Spirit that is constantly making itself known? There's no TV, no friends, no distractions except, "Uh, I think I'll go walk to that rock over there—or maybe over there? SRDD," I say to myself—which means, "Same rock, different day!"

It's funny how the Spirit makes itself known by holding up a mirror and showing me myself. And slowly but surely, it is working. In my own face I see It.

As I'm sitting on the edge, I'm less fearful, and it's obvious that "less fear inside equals less fear outside."

"You only have two more days to jump," I say to myself. "So if you're going to do it . . .

"I've been jumping over the edge since I got here," I say to my temptress. "And it wasn't about jumping over the edge. It never was. It was about hitting bottom. I just wanted to hit bottom.

"But there is no bottom," I add. "There are only the bottoms I've made for myself."

My temptress remain silent, as though she has been outma-
neuvered by something she can never understand.

"The Jordan River is not a river," Ya'el had said the week before,
after I told her I wanted to go there before I left Israel.

"When I went there last week," she continued, "I had to lie
facedown in it just to get a little wet. Parts of it are closed, and
the tourists can't even go to the usual place because it's too dry."

"I don't care if it's down to a trickle," I said. "I just want to
touch the same water Jesus did."

Later Mikael said, "That would be perfect for you: forty days
in the desert, then my apple strudel, then a dip in the Jordan,
and then you get on the plane back to the States."

Before my last prayer/meditation of the day, I thought of the
church where I had been an altar boy. It was the church my
mother often took me to for 6:00 a.m. Mass during the week. I
remember being there with her, how much it meant to her, and
how there usually were only two or three other people at the
6:00 a.m. service in a church that seated more than seven hundred people. I've decided to go there as soon as I get back to the
States in three days. It will be a Thursday—midday—when I
get back, so the church probably won't be open, but the
congregation built a lavish six-bedroom house next door for the
two priests. So I thought I'd go knock on their door.

"Hi," I'd say. "I'm sorry to bother you, but I was an altar boy at Our Lady Mother of the Church thirty years ago, and I was wondering if you could let me into the church for just a few minutes so that I could sit and pray."

"Excuse my appearance," I'd add. "I just came back from Israel, where I spent forty days in the Judean desert."

As I often do, I am hoping that the honesty in my heart and on my face will help convince the priests to open God's house to a man they've never met before.

In my prayer session, I was taken back to that church and to all my childhood friends. I saw all their jubilant, kind, and innocently open faces. I cried at having lost them after my parents died. We played so many kid games together . . .

Then I found myself being taken down the street where I lived. Whenever I've gone near that neighborhood in the past, I've gotten scared. And I was scared now, even though I was halfway across the world. I was still afraid of a place that meant so much to me.

I saw the wide streets where we played baseball. It was my favorite sport. I saw my house, and as I got closer, I cried even more deeply. I saw our garage and remembered I used to throw the ball endlessly against the brick face, which was just above the garage door. I loved doing such a simple thing. I saw myself putting my glove on the front step and going inside.

"Mom, I'm home," I said—as my mom came over to hug me. My dad, looking as heavy (both physically and spiritually) as ever, was seated in the kitchen.

The memory of that security, that love, that childhood time

was so dear to me. I wept more as I felt my childhood ripped away from me. Both of my parents died in a period of six months, and then I was no longer a child. I wasn't an adult either—I was something else that I still can't describe. I wept harder at the realization of what I'd lost. A time that I can never get back. And I saw that baseball mitt still sitting on the front step. Even a game that I loved so much lost its worth.

Finally, I felt my stomach swell up as though a baby were being born. And out of my mouth came a cry that I never would have uttered in public, a cry so deep that the lining of my soul turned inside out. I wept as I saw the "For Sale" sign out front. I stood in the house where my parents once lived, where I had lived, where my sisters lived—and the furniture was gone because my brothers and I had moved everything out. The house was vacant. Empty.

And then the cry came from an even deeper place, and I didn't know how I could ever allow it out. But then I thought of Jesus. I went into his arms and I let all my tension, all my holding back, all the skills I had used to survive—I let them all go while being held in his arms.

I cried myself free in the arms of Jesus.

I cried myself free into the arms of love.

I cried myself free into eternity.

And I was able to cry in his arms because he said, "I know . . . I know what it's like. I really know."

I cried what I knew into what he knew.

And there was no end to what I knew, and there was no end to what he knew. And they met in a place of peace.

After I washed off, I stood out in the desert. Last night I sang "I Get Around" by the Beach Boys. Even the stars applauded me, though I heard some "boos" from some minor moons around Jupiter.

Tonight I sang "My Sharona" by The Knack and then "It's Your Thing (Do What You Wanna Do)" by the Isley Brothers. Then I danced—feeling very open, loose, and free in every part of my body. As I danced I made up my own song:

If you're full of rhythm, then you're full of life.
If you're full of life, then you're full of rhythm—
Because life has rhythm, and rhythm is life . . .

As my *Soul Train* session slowly wound down, I walked farther onto the plateau for my nightly talk with the Big Guy.

"Yep," I said. "I'm feeling pretty good.

"I suppose I should thank you . . .

"No," I said emphatically. "I will thank you for my life. Right at this moment I'm glad I'm alive—and glad that you gave me life.

"At this moment, I don't know about the future or about the past. I just know about right now, this moment, and I'm glad I'm here and alive. Thank you."

day 39

It's morning, and the geckos are chasing each other above my mosquito net. That's when I heard something hit the ground next to me. I looked, but I didn't see a fallen gecko. Five minutes later I grabbed my backpack and opened it, and a gecko jumped out and landed on me. Instinctively, I jumped back and shook him off.

"You scared the heck out of me!"

It's so hot here, even on an average day like today. I have a plastic container of moist towelettes that I use to clean my hands after I go to the toilet. A few times previously when I went to use the towelettes, the top was half off.

"Bill," I scolded myself. "You have to be more careful with putting the top on right—otherwise, all the moist towelettes will become 'dry' towelettes."

Today, after using a towelette and putting the plastic canister back in my tent, I heard a *pop*. I realized that the heat has been popping the top off, and it hasn't been due to my being careless about it.

Boy, I'm a little disappointed in myself. I've survived the heat, bugs, snakes, scorpions, uncomfortable rock surroundings, passing out, and going over the edge of the cliff three times—but I'm getting a zit in the middle of my forehead, and it's bumming me out. After all I've been through these past forty days, and then to see that my vanity has survived. I wanted to step off the plane in three days and have my family and friends amazed at the light and obvious God presence coming from the glow around my face—not focused on an unusually large and prominently placed zit. See, that's how crazy people are—or how crazy I am. I don't think of loving them when I get off the plane; no, I think of how they will be either impressed or disappointed with how I look. What an idiot I am.

I don't know how I got this way. This concern with looks. All I know is when I started going bald when I was eighteen years old, it freaked me out. But I have to laugh, because sometimes I feel, as the Grateful Dead said, "set up like a bowling pin." As though the Spirit set an ego trap for me. When I asked my psychic friend, "Why did I have to go bald?" she laughed, as though sharing a joke with the angels in heaven, and said, "Sometimes God comes knocking at the front door and there's no answer. So he goes around to the back door and knocks. But there's still no answer. So he has to go in through the roof, and when he does, he knocks off a few shingles."

And that was so true. My appearance was where I took my

final stand in my last effort to get what I needed from the world and the people around me. But I learned that I will never, ever get all of what I need from the world. The world satisfies only the worldly part of me, but it takes Spirit to satisfy the Spirit in me. And that's why if a person seeks spiritual fulfillment from the world, it will never be enough; it will always be found lacking. That is what an addiction is: trying to fill a spiritual need with worldly devices such as alcohol, drugs, sex, relationships, food, television, and on and on. But if a person has a relationship with Spirit, then all the things of the world become extensions of the Spirit and reflect Spirit.

I'll say it for the umpteenth time: that's why I came to the desert—to connect more deeply with Spirit and to bring that Spirit into my world.

My two bird friends came four times today. It's nice to have friends, but it's also annoying. I can hear their babies screech that horrible screech, and it feels as though someone is holding a match to my nerve endings. But that screech is an example of karma! Because the two older birds will sit and screech at me and say other bird things until I feed them. And then when they return home, those baby birds yap, tweet, and do their baby screeching until they're fed. So what those two adult birds do to me gets done to them, and that's karma!

Those two birds also act coy. I will be holding out a piece of bread and calling them, but they sit on a ledge ten feet away and look every direction but at me! They know I'm there. They know I have food—but the birds don't want to appear to need me too much. It's like a man who used to be wealthy but isn't anymore. He needs help from a friend, but he's too proud, and instead of being honest and saying, "I need this," he waits for you to offer the money. Then after you offer it, he says, "No thanks," and just when you think he's not going to take it—just as you turn to leave—he grabs the money and says, "Okay," and never gives you the look of gratitude, because to be that open, real, and present, would threaten his conception of who he thinks he is. And those annoying birds are like that—proud.

In prayer/meditation, sometimes I'm like that bird and like that ex-rich man. I sit in the presence of God and look everywhere but where he is. If God always is, where can I hide? I hide in was and will be—past and future. The tension in my mind, body, and soul is mostly caused by holding on to what was or reaching for what will be. The amazing thing is that when I look directly at who I am, I begin to see who God is.

To truly know what you're doing inside and out, you must know who you are. Because in the depths of ourselves, in that place where our individuality dissolves into the love and Being of God, come the understanding and acceptance that are needed when seeing all that we, as human beings, do: the manipulations of others, the self-deceit, the self-centeredness. Our darkness can be seen only when we know our love.

But if you don't know who you are and yet say, "I know what I'm doing," everything you do is really done from within the shadow of ego and fear, because the deceits and manipulations are too painful to see without knowing your deep love. Your true motivations will never be known, because the beginning of your soul is lost in the shadows and not seen in its own light of love. That's why Jesus said, "Father, forgive them, for they do not know what they do" (Luke 23:34 NKJV). But herein lies the quandary: human beings cannot allow themselves to see their beginning if their beginning is but a shadow, because a shadow knows it will cease to exist the moment it's really seen. So how do human beings ever become free from fear? Or, as the apostles asked, "who then can be saved?"

"With man this is impossible, " Jesus said, "but not with God; all things are possible with God" (see Matthew 19:25–26).

day 40

I walked to the edge of the cliff above my cave.

"Brothers!" I yelled to the rocks and boulders in the canyon. Then I started to cry because I was leaving my teachers and friends. They were tears of gratitude toward all the participants of the last forty days. But I didn't cry long because the flies attacked me.

"I will almost even miss you," I said.

Then I heard the flies say something.

"What was that you said?" I asked, listening more closely.

"Oh—my mistake!" I said, hearing them clearly for the first time in forty days. "I didn't realize you weren't here to frustrate me right now—you were actually here to say, 'Good-bye'!"

Then I went to the edge of the cliff and stood there. The sun was shining directly in my face. I squinted my eyes and noticed I was standing more upright than I remembered. A new appreciation had been born in me. I was standing exactly how my friend Dave used to stand whenever he surveyed his natural surroundings—with his chest out and exposed. I actually felt his presence for a moment.

"It's like you're seeing through me, Dave," I said.

"I am seeing through you, Bill," Dave replied.

At sundown yesterday I stood in the canyon and started to clap.

"Lets hear it for the rocks and the cliffs," I said.

"And the birds over there," I said while clapping and pointing to their nest high up on the cliff. "You were good friends to have here, and I think you two birds have a better relationship than just about any human couple I know.

"Oh yes," I said to a swallow who flew nearby, "I enjoyed you swallows, too, even though we didn't get to know each other that well.

"And the snakes," I said, continuing to clap. "It was good to see you. Thanks for not biting me. Same with the scorpions; I saw only two small ones, but thanks for not hassling me.

"The sky! Let's hear it for the sky!

"And the sun! You burned away all that needed to be burned away.

"The mice and ibex, thank you.

"The flies and mosquitoes and biting red ants . . . well, I guess it was nice meeting you.

"And you all did a great job! Thank you for helping me!"

Last night, it was hard to fall asleep because it felt as though electric currents were running up and down my legs.

Also, while on a walk at dusk, I stumbled upon three very old ibex. One had twenty bumps on his horn, which meant he was twenty years old. I noticed that he was the only one who had a bare spot devoid of hair in the middle of his back. Then I saw him bend his head back so that his horn touched his back in the exact spot where it was bare. Then he swiveled his head from side to side and scratched his back with his horn!

I wondered what went through his mind. Since his horns are curved in such a way that he never sees them, what does he think is scratching his back? Sure, he can see other ibex with horns, but does that mean he's able to deduce that that thing on his head—that he can't see—is a horn? Why is he the only one with a bare spot on his back? Is he the only one who's figured out that he can scratch his own back?

It was a bit like the psychiatric hospital where I worked. Many patients were depressed and felt unloved, and yet whenever they had a visitor, such as a child or a pet dog, you could see the love they had for another coming out of their hearts—like a light shining outward. But for some reason, they couldn't take that same love they had for another, coming out of them like a beam of light, and turn it onto themselves. They seemed unaware of the love they possessed, just like the ibex who couldn't see their own regal horns. Except for the one ibex, who somehow knew of his own horns and used them to scratch his own back.

The psych patients who got better—really better, not just enduring their existence—were the ones who had the capacity to love themselves as well as another. They knew how to scratch their own backs with the loving hearts they had.

When Jesus admitted he was "the anointed one" (see Luke 4:18), he was admitting only to his own regal love, which curved about his head and heart. He emerged from the barren countryside filled with this knowledge and said, "I am in you— and you are in me" (see John 14:20), and "What I have done, you can do and more" (see John 14:12), so that we would believe we were as He, even if we couldn't see it for ourselves.

Then while washing a friend's feet, Jesus said, "I have set you an example" (John 13:15). Was it an example of how to wash another's feet? No, of course not. Jesus's whole life was his example to us. His being "the Anointed," "the Son of God," and "the Son of Man" was all done to show us who he is and who we are. To believe anything less about Jesus or ourselves makes his words smaller, not larger; makes his love smaller, not larger; makes the meaning of his life smaller, not larger.

If you allow Jesus's words into your heart, they become like a prairie fire that burns clear through to a new frontier in the Being of God.

I've been throwing bread to my bird friends, but then they started coming around all the time and bugging my meditation. At first I made their annoyance and screeching another part of my prayer.

But I'm not that great of a meditator, so I threw them larger pieces of bread, thinking that they could take a big piece home and enjoy it with the whole family while sitting on the couch— maybe they'd even relax and put their little bird feet up. But I discovered that if the piece was too big, they couldn't carry it. So they would only eat what they could and fly away, leaving the bread to dry out in the sun.

Maybe the Spirit that infuses all life is like that too. It tries to give us just enough so that we can digest it. If we're given too much, we're overwhelmed, and we'll just leave it in the sun to dry up and blow away.

I'm feeding the birds everything I have. They need to enjoy and fatten up while they can; there will be plenty of fasting after I'm gone.

I don't know whether to thank God, nature, the wind, or blind luck. For the last forty days everything's been fine despite winds I thought sure would rip open my tent. But today, on the fortieth day, I just climbed up to the plateau to get something out of my tent and found it blown over and ripped open in four or five places! One hole is so big I could almost use it as another door.

Is it just a coincidence that the wind waited until the last day to destroy my tent? I doubt it. There's a message there, and I think it's saying, "I've taken it easy on you for forty days, so tomorrow get your butt home to the States and don't ever come back!"

I spent the next hour duct-taping my tent together in the hot sun. The intense heat and wind had dried out the tape, and it was peeling off. I pinned the tape and tent together with Dave's camping clothespins. I only needed to keep the mosquitoes, scorpions, mice, snakes, and biting red ants out for one more night.

In Christian terms, during my prayer/meditation sessions, I'm mainly dealing with "the worldly" and the Spirit. "The worldly" includes everything from material things to thoughts, emotions, feelings, and the body. The Spirit is, of course, our soul, our "self," our true Being. "The kingdom of God that is within us," as Jesus said (see Luke 17:21).

So I just sit and watch the worldly things come and go in my Spirit. Often I am pulled into the worldly things, whether they're images or stories or thoughts or tensions. Then I just recognize what is taking place, and I allow them to do whatever they came to do. I don't embrace or reject them.

Slowly I sink more into Spirit, and as Spirit, I watch the worldly. As Spirit, I am free to enter into a relationship of freedom with the world, and not one of bondage or obsession. Relaxed into Spirit, my soul is not split in several directions or distracted by unconscious obsessions with the worldly, so when I choose to relate with my emotions, thoughts, or body, it can be even more fully done.

"Kiss me again and again, for your love is sweeter than wine."
—*Song of Songs 1:2* NLT

My prayer/meditation still has crying in it, but it's increasingly filled with a lot of pleasurable ecstatic energy. The first sign that it's present is when I start fantasizing about women.

I'll be halfway through a fantasy before I realize that I'm fantasizing. Then I'll stop myself and redirect my thoughts. The fan-
tasies are really a result of the ecstatic energy, and today after I
stopped being taken away by the fantasy, a deeper ecstasy
erupted. For the next forty minutes I was in a constant state of
extreme awareness.

The energy just mushroomed; it spasmed into every corner
of my Being and body. A couple of times the energy caused my
arms to go straight over my head; many muscle fibers and joints
snapped and crackled. At points my hands were blown open by
the energy, and I felt intense pleasure in each of my fingers. The
energy was like electric shocks, shooting across my palms and
along my fingers to my fingertips. Other times my head went
straight back, my mouth opened, and I felt hollowed out within
while simultaneously filled by an expansive and pure Presence.
My body was thrown back against the cave wall by energetic
spasms that erupted in and throughout my body and beyond. I
was very aware of not grasping at the extreme pleasure, but I
allowed it to do what it wanted. This ecstasy was not localized.
It was everywhere and rushed into every place.

Midway through the experience, I was aware of the possibility of being lost in the energy, of the pleasure hijacking my
awareness. But I gave myself to it anyway, without losing
awareness of what was happening. I experienced many different
levels, intensities, and sensations of energy. It dawned on me
that I was being shown them, and as the pleasure changed
direction and frequency, I adjusted and oriented freely within it.

At one point, I looked at Jesus's presence and wondered if he
was judging me and this ecstatic experience. But all I saw and
felt from him was love, without a speck of judgment. Then I

went back into the experience, and at the end I presented my being and my open, all-pervading sexuality to Jesus. He joyfully called me "brother." Then I was aware of being in God's presence as a sexual being; I experienced total love and acceptance. I felt the words "my son" throughout my being.

DUSK

My last meditation/prayer on the fortieth day and night was mainly a matter of being so happy that I cried great tears of gratitude. There was still the fear that I wouldn't be allowed to live this happily; that maybe even while praying, I'd drop dead.

The wind was the strongest it had been since my arrival. It was hard praying because small bits of stone were flying through the mosquito net and hitting me. As my forty days came to an end, I felt hollowed out—not hollowed out as in "nothing inside and dead feeling," but hollowed out as in all the old remnants of me that were no longer needed and actually had been in the way were gone. I felt full of Spirit.

Jesus said, "You don't put new wine in old wineskins, because it will burst the old skins and you'll lose the new wine. No—you put new wine in new wineskins" (see Matthew 9:17).

In the same way, I didn't put new Spirit in an old way of being or thinking or feeling, because that would have ruined both. Instead, the old me was hollowed out until it was gone, and then the new Spirit flowed into a newly born way of Being. This new Spirit expanded into and inhabited a new house without the limitations of the old house.

Despite the gusting winds, which one moment blew in one direction, then changed, swirling and blowing in the opposite,

I went down to the edge one last time. It was so windy that I thought, *What if a big and sudden wind blows me over the edge and I die?* I lessened that possibility by literally crawling on my hands and knees to the edge. Then I took a small scrap of paper out of my pocket and dropped it over the cliff. The wind pulled it this way and that as it fluttered all the way down, hitting bottom.

On the scrap of paper I had written, "Yes, one day I will die, but till then, I will live with a heart as big as the desert—and the desert has no beginning and no end."

DEPARTURE

I looked down at my leg, and there was a Jericho fly getting ready to bite me. You can't mistake them for a common fly, because Jericho flies are twice as big as a fly and look like a German WWII desert tank: armored and sand colored. Luckily, this was only the second one I had seen since my arrival.

I swiped at the fly with my hat and couldn't tell if I got him or not, but I wasn't sticking around to find out. Jericho flies give nasty bites and suck your blood like a vampire while laying eggs in your bloodstream. Any other questions?

It was hard sleeping last night. I was excited about going home, seeing my friends, my family, and Bonnie. In the past Bonnie and I were in a committed relationship, and even though we aren't committed to each other at this point, we're still very close and loving. So I've been wondering if she met someone while I was gone. It would be hard for me if she did, and if she didn't, it will still be hard for us as we figure out what our future is. Either way, it will be fantastic to see her and to share the desert with her. As she likes to say, "I'm closer to her than her jugular vein."

Down by the edge, there's a rock I always sat on. I scratched some words on it.

"Bill was here."

"Don't sit here or you will explode!"

"Bonzo [my nickname for Bonnie] was here too."

I also etched a little picture of a grass hut on stilts with a volcano in the background and the word *Hawaii* underneath. It was a scene I had first seen in a "teach yourself to draw" book when I was seven or eight years old, and since then I had sketched that picture hundreds of times.

I debated whether or not to carve on that rock—whether I was desecrating the rock and the desert. But I considered it a form of art like the ancient cave paintings, and besides, I felt the desert in me—it was closer to me than my jugular vein—and it was in this spirit of union that I etched upon that rock. But truth be told, come next winter, when the rains flood the desert and the rushing waters crash through and around my cave and forcefully take everything farther down toward the edge and over that cliff where I had sat for the last forty days—when that flood comes, the rock upon which I left my mark will be gone, and all evidence of my being in the desert will also be gone. And the hills will be silent and still, just as they were before I arrived.

Got up at 6:00 a.m. and packed. Once outside my tent, the flies and mosquitoes attacked. Then I remembered why I slept in every day till 7:00 a.m. The mosquitoes were vicious till the sun came out, heating up the desert and chasing them away. But that same sun heated up the sleeping flies—that was their alarm clock. That's why I had planned my exits from my tent accordingly; otherwise, if I left my tent at the wrong time, say between 6:30 and 7:15 a.m., then both the flies and the mosquitoes were active.

Made some tea for breakfast along with my last can of tuna. Believe it or not, the sweet tea and tuna were a real treat.

My big zit's going away, so I'll get to have a glowing face like Moses after coming down from the mountain—instead of having a glowing face with a big pimple in the middle.

I know what Bonnie would have done as soon as I got off the plane.

"Buddy, what's that?" she would have said playfully, simultaneously pointing out my pimple and my vanity.

By the way, the tea tastes a little funky because I don't wash cups very well. Also, the pot I boiled the water in had old crusty noodles and couscous stuck to the bottom. Boiling kills germs, doesn't it?

I went back under my mosquito net for a few hours, having already torn off the tarp that had been taped over the stones on the floor. I pulled it off because I did a typical "Bill" thing last night as I was leaving the cave.

Before my last prayer/meditation, I made a cup of coffee, and it was so good that I celebrated and made a second cup. My plan was to drink it after my prayer session, but during my meditation the wind blew so strongly that it sprayed me with stone bits and sand. I had to cover the coffee cup with something to keep out the flying debris. I placed my hat over the cup, and after the meditation session I reached for my hat—while forgetting about the coffee underneath—and you guessed it . . . coffee, cream, and sugar all over the tarp. The red ants would have feasted on that sugary caffeine and had an all-night "rave" party.

Since I pulled up the tarp, I'm lying and sitting on only a quarter-inch pad over stones. It looks very earthy and primitive and takes me back to how I felt when I first got here.

My two bird friends just got here, but I have no bread today. I left it here last night, and the wind blew it away, or perhaps an animal took it. But the birds are coming to within a foot or two of me and saying, "Hey, how about some food! Hey, buddy, remember us? You've been giving us food!"

"I don't have any," I replied. But it's no use—they're hanging around and waiting.

"Okay," I said, "I'll go down the canyon and look for the bag of bread."

I climbed down naked—and barefoot. I was really getting used to this naked thing, and I remembered how I tried to follow the ibex naked. How I danced under the stars and in the moonlight naked. And how Mikael, Tamir's roommate, had said, "You look wild!" And it was true—I felt wild, but it wasn't a wild out of control; it was a natural wildness. The irony being that by letting go and being totally wild, I was actually more in control of myself than ever.

I couldn't find the bread, so I went back to my cave empty-handed.

All morning I've been talking to the birds. I know more bird language than Hebrew. I know "A-Rickia-Heard?" and "R-We-Ree?"

and the shortened forms they sometimes say: "A-Rickia?" or "R-We?"

One day, after I had heard "A-Rickia-Heard?" for the umpteenth time, I couldn't stand it anymore, and I blurted out, "I think A-Rickia's heard by now! And if he hasn't heard by now, he isn't gonna—so shut up!"

Even the plants "bite" here! Yesterday I put my hand down on my meditation pillow during the windstorm, and ouch! A seed with thorns attached had been blown into my cave. This morning when I woke up, the two fingers still hurt and had scabbed-over puncture marks.

The cries of my two bird friends' hungry babies got to me. I climbed out of my cave and up to the plateau where I dug some old dates out of the garbage pile forty yards from my tent. Then I went back down to my cave, but the birds were nowhere in sight. I spotted them on a cliff across the canyon. I held up the bag and shook it and made some birdcall noises. They flew over to me, and I tossed the dates their way. They grabbed the dates in their beaks, talking happily as they flew off together.

I spent my last prayer/meditation praying for everyone I knew. I brought each person into "the top of my heart." It's a weird

way of saying it, because it's actually the place where you concentrate and it's in the middle of your forehead. Some people
call it "the mind's eye"—but I don't care for that idea because it
makes it sound as though it's intellectual and not connected to
my heart. Being in the desert for forty days has allowed me to
drop the separation between mind and heart, and as Stephen
Levine said, "Where there's no mind, there's only heart." So it
was from "the top of my heart" that I prayed, "May you feel
loved," "May you be loving," and "May you be happy."

Love, of course, changes everything. To be loved is tremendous,
but it's the awareness of being loved—the feeling that you're
loved—that is the ultimate comfort. Something in a person
relaxes when they experience "being truly loved." I knew I was
loved here in the desert—that is in part what allowed me to come
here. Even Jesus went into the desert only after he heard God say
he was loved, and I did the same. I came here because the love
that Jesus felt had also driven me into the desert—like a moth to
the flame. This faith, this love, allowed me to relax everything in
myself that had resisted life and divided it up. This life undivided
is what Jesus called "a life in full" (see John 10:10).

I also prayed for everyone I didn't know.

I left the cave and took down the tent. It was probably another
day over 130 degrees in the sun. It took an hour and a half to
pack up my gear, together with all the unique rocks I've collected, the ibex horn, the porcupine quill, and the key. I walked
around and collected garbage—even picking up some garbage I
knew wasn't mine.

There was one thing left to do, and that was make good on the promise I made to the bees about digging them a water hole. I grabbed my stainless-steel bowl, the one I had eaten out of for the last forty days, and a spoon. I climbed down to my cave and started digging right next to it.

Within ten minutes I was soaked with perspiration. And the water level? It must have dropped, because I dug deeper than the original hole and still no water! Finally, I quit—exhausted by the digging, packing, and cleaning up I had done in the hot morning sun. Frustrated, I threw the bowl and spoon up ahead of me and then climbed back up to the plateau.

I grabbed the cell phone from my backpack and called Ya'el, asking her to tell Tamir to bring a shovel with him. Dehydrated and tired, I stumbled back to my cave in a fog and dropped onto the mat under my mosquito net. The heat, together with my wet, sticky perspiration-soaked clothes, and the fact that I was waiting for Tamir to pick me up so that I could start my journey home, made the time move very slowly.

Sitting up, I drank the last of my water, and as I lay back down I said, "Well, Tamir—you'd better show up; else I'm a dead man."

After a while, I heard the sound of a car pulling up.

"Free at last . . . ," I said.

When I climbed out of the cave to meet Tamir, I saw that he had a young man with him.

"I brought you extra digging help," Tamir said, carrying a shovel. "This is Ya'el's son, Gil."

Then Gil smiled, and just like his mother, the smile filled his face. We talked for a few minutes, with Gil making every effort to accommodate me with his limited English vocabulary.

The three of us descended down to the cave. I took the

shovel and started digging. Gil sat in the shade and watched, while Tamir took down my mosquito net.

I wanted to be the one to dig this water hole and give my hornet friends a good-bye present. But like Sidney Poitier in *Lilies of the Field*, I discovered I couldn't do it alone. I stopped after ten or fifteen minutes of digging, exhausted and sweaty.

"You want . . . ," Gil asked while searching for the right words, "that I should dig?"

"Yeah," I said, handing him the shovel. I gave him a warm pat on the back and he dug, but he didn't last long either in the hot sun, so Tamir started digging.

"I can smell it," Tamir said. He dug faster and more intensely than either Gil or I—but the water hole's sand walls kept collapsing and continually filled up the hole. Tamir was hardly getting anywhere. I climbed back up to the plateau, got the stainless-steel bowl, and brought it back to the dry water hole. I scooped out the stony sand, and then it began; water seeped in through the walls while also rising up from the bottom. It had taken close to forty minutes, and we had to go much deeper and wider than before—but now there was water where there had been none before. I guess the truth is that it was there all along; it just needed to be uncovered.

I watched Tamir drive away with all my gear. I had decided to walk out of my desert, not be driven out. The sun rose higher in the sky as I walked along. Halfway up the first ridge, my hip began to hurt. It was an old injury from playing with my father as a child. It hadn't bothered me for years, but it started to hurt a few days before I went into the desert. During my forty days, it never hurt once, and I had forgotten that I had ever hurt it at all.

Once I got over the ridge, the pain disappeared and I stopped limping. I made a detour and kicked over the bedouin stone markers I had set up for Ya'el in order to show her the way to my cave when she delivered my weekly supply of water.

"Those markers would draw tourists and their four-wheel-drives to your cave," Tamir said. "It wouldn't be a good thing for the cave or the environment."

As I walked through the last valley and got closer to the hostel, I came upon more and more trash: broken glass, cast-out cans, plastic bags blown against desert plants and caught in their branches, and hundreds of spent rifle casings. Civilization had thrown its trash into the desert with hopes of making itself clean, but all it had done was extend itself farther into the desert.

When I reached the barbed-wire fence that surrounded the hostel, I turned and looked back at where I had just come from. My eyes welled up with tears of gratitude toward the desert and all that lived in the desert; but most of all my tears were for myself, because there was a time in my life when I had so little—and now, I had so much.

acknowledgments

In some ways it is hard to thank a handful of people, because so many have helped me. I, like many people, am blessed to feel the inspiration and direction of Spirit, but along with that blessing comes a curse, because often the world (and even ourselves) is at odds with what inspiration demands we do. It is true that Spirit will often carry us, and to some extent one's own sense of faith and will contribute also. But there is always the dark night of doubt that must come, because only this can teach us the lesson that comes from having friends answer the call when we cannot. Of course, they are not called *to fulfill* our destiny for us; instead, they are called *to support* that which they have come *to love and respect*. It has been at moments such as these that I am humbled and wonder, *What have I done to deserve such love?*

I want to thank my dearest friend, Bonnie Milgrim, for supporting me in so many ways through the years. You encouraged, loved, and believed in me (sometimes more than I believed in myself).

I would like to thank Marge Rolfing for helping me

remember my connection to soul, spirit, and inspiration whenever the weight of the world became too much.

Andy Moore, thank you for our friendship and our soul sharing. Thanks to Mike Casali for the heart talks. Pat McBride, Michael Blatnik, and Nur'un'nisa for sharing their time and gifts with me.

Mike Bernarde and Ty, I am grateful for the long, deep friendship.

I am indebted to my sister Diane, who took me in after our parents died, and Mary, Liz, Jim, and Ed, who are the greatest brothers and sisters in the world.

Dave DuRose for being my friend and teaching me that there are different ways to live and perceive other than those we are born into.

Thanks to the desert and spiritual guides Tamir Ya'ari and Ya'el Mey-Orah for taking me into the desert and showing me how beautiful and full the desert is even when it is empty. And thanks to Rabbi Zalman Schachter and Rabbi Ohad Ezrahi and the Hamakon movement at http://www.hamakom.org.il/.

Thanks to Don Shmauz for being a generous and gifted healer.

Thanks to my friends Jim Kramlinger, Mark Hottman, Fran Breit, Greg Mondin, Sue Joy Sobota, Steve Stein, and Loren Mortenson for giving me a heartfelt mulligan once in a while . . .

Thanks to Roger Peasley (for all the heart-to-heart, soul-revealing talks we have had) and Julie Alexander for friendship and transcription, Michelle Prentice, Ernie E & S Auto, Becca, Hugh and Gayle, Chris Moore, Dru, Jack, Greta, Ursula Hermacinski, Martin, Todd, Jacques, Pamela Minden, Janice, and Bruce Winkka.

Thanks to Dave Phillips for wilderness tips. Mickey Milgrim, I miss you. And Lex.

I am grateful to Jane Alden, Bill Cheadle, Sandy, Angela Smith, and Mark Sweet for reading my manuscript and giving compassionate criticism. It is hard finding *balanced* feedback.

To Matt Flickstein for answering the call to mirror true nature, and to Chokyi Nyima for helping me relax into it.

Kak Dorgan, Howie Cohn, Henry Brockman, Rich Beilfuss, Robin Daley and Bill, Atum, Aziza, Mary Inayat, Mark Chimsky, Judith Estrin, Mary Laird, and Shahabuddin.

Joe Sonza, Barb, Brent, Cindy McCallum, Dooley, Jim G., Patrick Jones, June, Jody, Roget, Terri, Teresa, Alison, Jeff and Eli, Karen K., Ed, David, Loren Mortenson, and Mary.

A special thanks to St. Benedict's Monastery in Snowmass: Father Thomas Keating, Pat Johnson, Mary Ann Matheson, and Father Micah Schonberger.

Thank you, Lindsey, and your Ground Zero coffee shop, for creating such a wonderful atmosphere for coffee drinking, writing, and meeting with friends.

To my friends at The Mental Health Center of Dane County: Karen, Al, George, Judy, Dave, Lori, Marcie, Maurie, Beth, Barb, Justice, Lee, Pattie, Marlin, Mary, Liz, Kristin, Jim, Deborah, Patricia, Sheila, Vicki, Gina, Tammy, Elsbeth, Nancy, Jane, Alex, and Bob.

To all my family: Ed, Laura and Dale, Rebecca and Dan, Jeff and Wanda, Keith and Kristine, Barb and Nate, Pat and Irish, Jen and John, Shannon and Brian, Chris, Jimmy and Lori, Jack, Jill and Tom, Jessie and Mark, Pat, Jolly, and Bobby, Dick and Kim, Carol, Margie, Uncle John and Carol, Uncle Bubbles, Tommy, Barb and Chuck, Marty and Kay, Joni, Phyllis and George.

And special thanks to Kate Etue, Adria Haley and David Moberg at W Publishing Group for being open-minded and having wise souls.

I am very grateful to Bob Schwartz (my friend and agent). I had often heard mythic and ancient stories about agents who helped edit their author's material, while also being a friend who offered encouragement, but I had never met one till I met Bob. Thank you for believing and for having the skills to make believing a reality.

To my mother and father, who continue to teach me thirty years after their death. She was loving, and he was tough; these two things helped me survive and thrive in the desert and in life.

And finally, to Susan Talarico, thank you for coming into my life. May our relationship continue to deepen in love, trust, and intimacy; and may your beautiful children, Nicolas, Anya, and Lenora, continue to be loved and loving. Pupino, too.

about the author

Bill Elliott is a therapist, author, and speaker who is on a personal and literary quest for meaning. He has traveled across America and around the world to interview legendary spiritual and religious figures, resulting in his critically acclaimed books, *Tying Rocks to Clouds* and *A Place at the Table*.

www.williamelliott.com